CONTENTS

FOREWORD *by H. Levy*   7

EDITORIAL NOTE *by T. A. Jackson*   15

INTRODUCTION   17

I. TWO WORLD OUTLOOKS   25

II. MATERIALISM: MECHANICAL AND DIALECTICAL   33

III. THE GENERAL NATURE OF DIALECTICS   43

IV. DIALECTICS OF SOCIETY   55

V. DIALECTICS AND LOGIC   65

VI. DIALECTICS AND SOPHISTRY   74

VII. THE PHILOSOPHICAL STRUGGLE TO-DAY   85

VIII. PROBLEMS OF SOCIALIST CULTURE   94

BIBLIOGRAPHY   101

A TEXTBOOK OF DIALECTICAL MATERIALISM

by David Guest

WITH A FOREWORD BY H. LEVY

Professor of Mathematics at the Imperial College of Science, London

NEW YORK

INTERNATIONAL PUBLISHERS

PRINTED IN THE U. S. A.

 72

A TEXTBOOK OF
DIALECTICAL MATERIALISM

FOREWORD

BY H. LEVY

In the summer of 1931 a crowded audience of historians
and scientists, interested in the history of their subject, listened
with close attention to a series of papers read by delegates from
the U.S.S.R., in a lecture room of the Science Museum, at
South Kensington.

To the great majority of those present the standpoint con-
sistently adopted by the speakers was a novel one, not easily
grasped by a British audience of confused philosophical outlook.
We were required to see scientific growth as an essential part
of social development, to see the contributions of the scientists
as the natural accretions to that growth as they strove to solve
the problems their society had thrown up, and so to enable
us to estimate the individual scientist, no matter how eminent,
in the social context in which he lived.

It was then that Hessen read his famous paper on Newton
that has since served as a model for so many studies of other
scientific men. The audience was a little uncomfortable; it
wished to give gentlemanly attention to what these foreigners
had to say; it could not believe that anything they could say
would be at all significant; but at the same time it found the
ideas presented to them so new and, from its point of view,
so revolutionary as to make it impossible to form a judgment
or to direct an intelligent attack. In short, at that particular
moment, except to those of us who had already begun to think
along these lines, the ideas were too novel to be absorbed, ap-
parently too outrageous to be seriously considered or discussed.
When the last speaker had finished and the time for discussion had arrived, those of us who might have spoken were

temporarily tongue-tied by the difficulty of bridging the wide gap that had been disclosed between the speakers and the great majority of the audience, who so far as it was prepared to be tolerant, was silent because the ideas were too strange.

At this awkward moment a pale-faced young boy, sitting behind me, bent over and whispered in my ear:

"Do you think I ought to speak?"

"Yes," I answered immediately, "if you have something to say," secretly delighted that someone from the English side should have the courage to make a contribution. And so this gawky lad stepped to the rostrum and quite easily, as if it were the most natural thing in the world, carried on the theme that had been expounded by "these foreigners."

In a short pointed speech he illustrated the general argument with reference to the outlook of English men of science, dealing in particular with Pearson and Russell. That was David Guest, and it was typical. At the critical moment he stepped into the breach feeling that the responsibility was his, and he carried it through triumphantly.

It is not easy for those who do not move in academic circles to visualise the forces at play in this and other situations connected with university life. The vilification of Russia that had so persistently been pursued in the National Press and that was being focused on the delegates during the congress, implied an atmosphere in which only a person who was prepared to espouse an unpopular cause and to throw his academic future to the winds would do battle. More than this; only a person of David's political understanding could appreciate that even the history of science and its discussion in that environment on that basis must make precisely the same types of demand upon his allegiance as would the more obvious major political issues. Only a person to whom the problem of poverty and the emancipation of the workers from wage slavery was a burning fire could feel called upon to make that decision and feel urged to act upon it on every occasion.

I knew David Guest as a young boy just before he went to Cambridge. I saw him at intervals throughout his undergraduate career, and I made close contact with him during the succeeding period. On every occasion the question that was uppermost in his mind was—in what way is the work which I am doing of assistance in solving this fundamental problem? His life was a perpetual struggle in that sense, for it meant that the natural desire which he shared with every intellectual person, to explore those fields of thought that might bring him personally mental pleasure, were to be denied him or to be turned towards coping with the problems of social progress. On no other terms could he have mental peace. In dialectical materialism David Guest found just this unification, and time and again he swung back to his mathematical studies or to certain aspects of those studies, always in the effort to transform them into tools for his other problems. He was no bourgeois student in whose eyes everything was subservient to his mathematical and personal career.

In a time of comparative social quietude this would have offered no insuperable task, but David Guest lived in a period of turmoil in which the problems of to-day have become so acute and have penetrated so deeply as to embroil every sensitive person. With a boy of his temperament therefore it was natural that his political activities should appear to gain at the expense of his mathematical studies. The consequence was that he would spend himself for many months on end, unsparingly, on political education at Marx House, or among the unemployed, until for a sensitive soul like himself the physical and emotional strain would become unbearable. He would then return to wrestle with philosophical errors of Bertrand Russell or to study the methods of teaching mathematics in such a way as to prevent the false idealism, latent in the orthodox approach, from poisoning the mind of the student.

I saw him in Russia where he had gone to recuperate after a particularly wearing spell. He sought me out in my hotel. Although I had not seen him for over a year, in two minutes he was deep in philosophy, translating passages for me out of a Russian work and discussing the subject of a paper he was writing for the journal *Under the Banner of Marxism* to which Lenin and so many other theoreticians had contributed.

David discussed Bertrand Russell and the Machists, the importance of coming to grips with the rising school of logical positivists in Vienna, and the ideas of Wittgenstein in Cambridge; he emphasised the danger of losing the essential parts of philosophy—those that were linked up with the day to day struggle—if one merely concerned oneself as they did, with verbal forms.

While recognising a value in the proper formulation of problems, as a good dialectical materialist he saw this as only one of the steps towards effective action. He pointed out the danger that the younger generation of scientists and philosophers might be lost to the active movement if they were side-tracked by a deficient and basically empty philosophy of this nature.

I was taken by David to see a *kolhoz*, or collective farm, about an hour's rail journey from Moscow. Fortunately, he knew exactly where to stand on the platform so that we were able to enter the incredibly crowded train during its short halt at the station.

We visited a children's crèche situated in the centre of a wood, a swimming pool, and an open-air theatre for plays, lectures, organisational discussion and radio. It was one of the "sixth day" holidays. A young peasant who had won a bicycle as a prize for good factory work was learning to ride on a footpath. He sought desperately to remain glued at an impossible angle to the seat of his machine. Every now and again I heard the thud, as he failed. He did not utter a sound but kept on trying with amazing persistence. I gave him "a hand" before continuing my walk with David. From the hill-side we looked down on the workers who were sitting about intent on their books.

"I'd like to know what they are reading," I said.

"Let's go and look," he suggested.

It was astounding. With the exception of one old woman everybody was reading technical works on mathematics, physics, mechanics and chemistry. David remarked humorously that he might have "stage-managed" it for my benefit!

It was getting dark as we returned to the station. Three middle-aged country labourers passed us talking earnestly. A fragment of their conversation reached us. "What a change ... don't you remember what the peasants were like a few years ago ... ignorant and superstitious ... ?"

It was characteristic of David that although he had gone to Russia to recover from over-work he should have found it relaxation, not only to study philosophy and to read it in the Russian, but to teach in a school. He was never the kind of theorist who would formulate his ideas in an abstract way in the isolation of a study, but always sought for ways to put them to the test. The meaning of this became obvious when he returned from Russia and settled in Battersea, carrying on propagandist education by running a series of classes on Marxism and establishing a bookshop. I can imagine what this must have meant in expenditure of energy knowing as I do something of his other activities.

He came to me with draft sets of lectures he was delivering on dialectical materialism, in which he was attempting to illustrate his points, not only from matter of current political importance but from many diverse fields of science.

The idea then took shape between us of working out a new

approach to the teaching of mathematics on dialectical lines; of dealing with students at the early stages and for this purpose recasting the scheme of instruction, so that the successive steps in the mathematical development would show themselves as arising each out of the internal limitations and contradictions of the earlier stages.

The background in the method was a sketch of the social setting in which the mathematics developed, as efforts were made to resolve the problems of a practical nature that presented themselves at each such social period.

But it was important also to recognise that this relation between mathematics and its social background was a dialectical and changing one. Thus the relationship would not always be a severely practical one—on occasion theoretical and even abstract problems of mathematical technique would emerge as of importance.

It became necessary to make clear how the struggle on the economic and social plane, and the confusion in that plane, were being reflected in struggles and confusions of a highly theoretical and abstract nature. In this David could bring to bear his very valuable knowledge of mathematical logic and his appreciation of the finer points around which there existed much confusion.

He took the matter very seriously, read a great deal and made copious notes. Some of the most enjoyable hours I have spent have been in discussing with him details of the projected text-book. There was one real difficulty. He found he had to rely on me for much of the practical teaching experience; and as a real dialectical materialist he could not be satisfied with confining himself purely to the theoretical aspect. I was not surprised therefore when he finally presented me with an ultimatum that he could not proceed until he had devoted more time to actual teaching. We can see how objective was his judgment and precise his self-criticism in such matters.

It was for that reason that I urged him to offer himself for a vacancy as a lecturer on mathematics at University College, Southampton.

At the time I lived in Winchester, only a few miles away, and was able to maintain contact with him while he was attached to the college.

His capacity to inspire others with something of his own enthusiasm is evident in the tributes from his friends on the staff.

The way in which David went to Spain was characteristic of his whole attitude. Having made up his mind, in spite of the attempts of certain of his friends to dissuade him, he carefully arranged all his affairs and quietly slipped off. It was not until he had actually reached the firing line that I learnt that he had gone.

A knowledge of mathematics is an asset in warfare, just as much of mathematical development has itself been evolved out of needs of war in the past. As an observer and topographer therefore, David found himself particularly useful, especially in relation to gun spotting and range finding. Moreover on the instructional side his specialised knowledge was an immediate asset to others less highly qualified than himself. It is related that at a military school some Spanish officers were trying to explain a rather complicated technical problem to a bewildered class. David came to the rescue and with a piece of chalk and a few strokes made the matter clear to the soldiers.

Even under the conditions at the front he lost no opportunity in awakening the interest of the Brigadiers in the subjects in which he had specialised—philosophy and mathematics. The extent to which this was appreciated is clear from a letter from a young worker:

"A few days before we crossed the Ebro, David and I got to discussing philosophy, or perhaps it would be better to say that I had a lecture on it. I knew that David was a brilliant mathematician, but I could not see clearly the role of mathematics in philosophy. He explained it to me: Math is not an exact science although for a general level of education in bourgeois society it is sufficient to satisfy the average demand. But in socialist society when there are no artificial limits imposed on learning and culture, this 'inexactness' is not in keeping with the new philosophy and cannot satisfy it.

"I am afraid that this is not very clear. I don't profess to understand the whole of the discussion despite David's patience in trying to drive it into me. . . .

"He was keen on his job and at all odd times he could be seen studying all kinds of text-books (procured I don't know how) to gain a better knowledge of his work."

David Guest and hundreds of other lads sacrificed their lives to atone for the blunders of the people at home. I could see in him the eternal conflict that tears asunder the souls of all that is best in the younger generation—the desire to enjoy the fruits of culture and the necessity to sacrifice oneself for its preservation. That such a dilemma should exist is one of the insanities of a stupid economic system.

How can one appraise a human being whom one knew so well and with whom one sympathised so closely? A rational and intelligent society would have known how to use his mental powers, his emotional fervour and his fineness of feeling. Released from the urgent tasks thrown up for him by a feverish raging capitalism, David Guest would have made his contributions to mathematics and philosophy. If the world of science is temporarily the poorer for his going, finally it must be the richer for his struggles.

Reprinted from *David Guest—A Scientist Fights for Freedom* (*1911-1938*), a commemorative volume edited by his mother, Carmel Haden Guest.

EDITORIAL NOTE

In preparing David Guest's manuscript for the press I have made only those alterations in the text—all of them purely verbal—which I felt sure he would himself have made. In one place a sentence—found to be unnecessary—was removed; in another a sentence was added. One quotation was removed and replaced by a more apposite one, and half a dozen footnotes have been added in places where it seemed they would be helpful.

Otherwise the work is just as David Guest left it. I did not feel it either necessary or desirable to alter those few passages which serve to date his work precisely, or those in which he is much too flattering to myself.

In the main, the work speaks for itself. It should do what he intended it to do, namely, lead plain men and women to a readier and a fuller understanding of the cause for which he gave his life.

T. A. Jackson

INTRODUCTION

The Need for Theory

How far can the working-class movement go without bothering about theory?

Even to-day we often meet practical workers who look on "theorising" as an interesting but not very important side-line, sometimes even regarding it with contempt as a waste of time. Indeed it is not impossible that someone with these views will pick up this little volume and skim the first few pages. If so, he will be bound to notice that it deals with some highly "theoretical" questions, and if we are to prevent him closing it impatiently we must attempt some sort of self-justification. In short, we must answer the practical man's questions, "What is the *use* of all this theorising?" and "How can it help a practical worker to *get on with the job?*"

The best way of doing this is to follow our friend the would-be practical worker in the "day-to-day" struggle. Whatever his field of activity he soon finds that at every turn he runs up against the much-despised theory. He finds himself forced to ask, "What do we do next?" And the answer always involves another question, "What result are you trying to achieve?" In order to justify his course of action on any particular matter (for example, a strike), he has to make an appeal to *general* grounds (in this case the general end desired and the *general* experience of strike tactics). But general statements of this kind make up precisely what we call *theory*—and if they have the further character of being checked up by experience we call them *scientific theory*.

The theory at the basis of all conscious Socialist activity is modern *Scientific Socialism* (*Marxism*). This comprises first

17

of all the strategy and tactics of the class struggle in the narrow sense (in which the strike tactics just mentioned are a detail). It requires also a knowledge of the historical economic roots of class divisions in capitalist society, and of those laws of development of capitalism which were first investigated by Marx in his great work *Capital*.

But capitalism has only existed during a part of human history, and human society and its history covers only a small part of the whole period that life has existed on the earth. Again, life on the earth has endured for only a very brief portion of the vast history of matter. All this compels us to attempt to see our problems in perspective—in relation to the world and its development as a whole. Only in this way can we be sure that we have not left something out of the picture, and that our method of investigation is the correct one.

The Proletarian World Outlook

What we are seeking is a *general view of the world* which shall be rooted in the facts of science—including here not merely the so-called "natural sciences" (physics, chemistry, biology, etc.), but also the sciences of human society and human thought. Without such a general view Scientific Socialism cannot be complete, cannot stand firmly on its own feet. The working out of such a "world outlook" or philosophy is all the more important because Scientific Socialism does not win universal acceptance in present-day (bourgeois) society. In fact its root assumptions conflict with the general outlook that dominates bourgeois society.

This *bourgeois world outlook* is in the first place conservative, and for that reason hostile to a scientific study of human society with all its revolutionary implications. In the second place, so far as form is concerned, it is most commonly *religious*, regarding the existing order as in some way divinely sanctioned. Even where not openly religious it retains certain anti-scientific features, exalting "mind" or "spirit" above "mere matter." Both the general picture of the world and the very technique of thinking are affected by that fear of passing beyond the limits of capitalism, which is most characteristic of the bourgeois outlook.

It is clear that this bourgeois outlook can only be a hindrance to the workers in their class struggle for emancipation. In order to free themselves from the chains of capitalism, chains which are mental as well as physical, the workers (whom we will call collectively the *proletariat*) need a militant, revolutionary philosophy. This philosophy must not be like the philosophies of the past, which as Marx said in his *Theses on Feuerbach*, "only *interpreted* the world in different ways," but it must actively guide and direct the proletariat in its revolutionary task of *changing* the world. It must be *materialistic* in the sense that it is based on scientific study of the material world, on an acceptance of this as the basic reality. But at the same time it must see this world in process of constant revolutionary change, it must be *dialectical*.

The development and application of this philosophy of *Dialectical Materialism*, which is the proletarian world outlook we have been seeking, forms the subject of this book. While in some ways it might seem to be the most "theoretical" of subjects, we have seen that it arises in response to definite practical needs. We will find later that it is a mighty and indispensable weapon on all fronts of the class struggle.

The Unity of Theory and Practice

It is not only in the social and political field that theory is seen to arise out of practice. A study of the history of the sciences shows how each science in turn has grown out of the knowledge gained in practice and out of the need to extend that practice to wider and more difficult fields of endeavour. As Engels says:

> "The *successive developments* of the separate branches of natural science should be studied. First of all, *astronomy*—if only on account of the seasons it was absolutely indispensable for pastoral and agricultural peoples. Astronomy can only develop with the aid of *mathematics*. Hence this also had to be tackled. Further, at a certain stage of agriculture and in certain regions (raising of water for irrigation in Egypt), and especially with the origin of towns, big building operations and the development of handicrafts—*mechanics*. This was soon needed also for *navigation* and *war*. Moreover it requires the aid of mathematics and so promotes the latter's development. Thus, from the very beginning the origin and development of the sciences has been determined by production" (Engels, *Dialectics of Nature*).

All scientific workers to-day recognise more or less fully that scientific theory grows out of social practice—is, in fact, a continuation of social practice "by other means"—and in turn reacts upon and aids the development of further practice.

In his essay on Newton (in *Science at the Crossroads*) Hessen brilliantly destroys the conventional idea of Newton as "Some dreamer of the skies," far removed from considerations of earthly practice. He shows how the problems solved by Newton were set by the "all-too human" practical needs of the time.

But if theory first arises in response to practical needs it must not be forgotten that once arisen it has its degree of independent development, and reacts, more or less powerfully, upon the practical basis from which it arose, and effects its developing transformation.

Thus theory and practice form a "unity of opposites" whose mutual modification has and can have no conceivable end while the human race endures. Human practice is primary—"In the beginning was the deed," as Goethe says—but since "practice makes perfect" its development forces forward the development of theory and this reacts back on the practice as we have already seen.

Recognition of this *unity of the "opposites" theory and practice* is the very keystone of Dialectical Materialism, and as we will see immediately is one of the points where it most sharply encounters bourgeois philosophy.

Theory and the Labour Movement

We have now to explain the peculiar attitude of many practical workers to theory that we noticed at the beginning. In part this attitude is a general result of class-divided society and due to the division of labour between "manual" and "intellectual" workers that capitalism has carried to the utmost limit. This division of labour leads to theory being developed in apparent independence of practice, and gives rise to scholastic, abstract, "armchair," theories which naturally excite the contempt of "practical" people. The "split" between theory and practice generated in this way is further intensified by the conservative limitations of bourgeois thinking, and that inability to face up to reality which is the cause of so much *hypocrisy* in bourgeois thought. The mental attitude involved in this split between theory and practice is far commoner than is realised, even among Socialists who think themselves free from bourgeois taint. It is crystallised in such a remark as "It may be true in theory, but it does not work out in practice." Against this sort of muddled thinking, which fails to see that the truth of a theory is tested in practice, we must declare merciless warfare. It is largely responsible for the contemptuous attitude of the practical worker to theory.

But part of the cause of this attitude in the British Labour Movement must be set down to specific "national" circumstances. Over sixty years ago Engels wrote of "the indifference of the English Labour Movement towards all theory, which is one of the reasons why it moves so slowly, in spite of the splendid organisation of the individual unions." [2] This relative indifference to theory and preference for rule-of-thumb, empirical methods was shared by the British workers with other classes of British society. It was undoubtedly the result of the early development of British capitalism which gave the bourgeoisie plenty to do exploiting its monopoly of the world market (in which the workers shared indirectly), and allowed it to leave to the less favoured continental bourgeoisie the consolation of theorising. When the modern Labour Movement came into existence on the basis of the craft unions it had this empirical character very strongly impressed on it. It could not of course get along completely without theory. But the theory it almost unconsciously adopted was the bourgeois Liberalism and Radicalism of the day. This was later dressed up as the Utopian idealist Socialism of the I.L.P., though in essence it remained on the same platform of humanitarian reform.

It took the shocks of the world crisis of Imperialism that began with the Great War to reveal the inadequacies of this "Socialism" and to show that the Scientific Socialism of Marx and Lenin was the only reliable guide for the Labour Movement. Since then the further developments of the crisis have shaken many people in all classes out of their state of mental inertia and have driven them to seek some explanation of *why* things are happening as they are. This is the secret of the growing popularity of all kinds of philosophy, psychology and pseudo-science.

The old attitude to theory is indeed breaking down. The practical man, the devotee of common sense, realises that the world is a more difficult place than he had thought. But there is a danger of his lapsing into the other extreme, of his embracing any kind of fantasy merely because it appears to offer some kind of explanation of the world. Only a scientific theory, one closely linked up with practice, deserves to be listened to. And the only world outlook which is based scientifically on the sum-total of available human knowledge is Dialectical Materialism.

I. TWO WORLD OUTLOOKS

The great basic question of all philosophy, especially of modern philosophy is that concerning the relation of thinking and being.[1] ENGELS.

Materialism versus Idealism

We have seen that the theoretical basis of the working-class movement—Scientific Socialism—implies a consistent, many-sided scientific outlook on the world. This outlook is incompatible with theological or mystical conceptions, in that it seeks a natural explanation of all phenomena, including the phenomena of human society. On this fundamental issue it comes inevitably into conflict with the dominant outlook of bourgeois society.

Here we have a conflict which is modern in form but in essence is very old. The point at issue is in fact what Engels calls "the great basic question of all philosophy." After showing that the source of this problem lies in the theological notion of the "soul," which derives ultimately from the naïve guesses of primitive peoples, Engels goes on to explain its modern form:

"The answers which the philosophers gave to this question split them into two great camps. Those who asserted the primacy of Spirit to Nature and, therefore, in the last instance, assumed world creation in some form or other—(and among the philosophers, Hegel, for example, this creation often becomes still more intricate and impossible than in Christianity)—comprised the camp of idealism. The others, who regarded Nature as primary, belong to the various schools of materialism.

"These two expressions, idealism and materialism, primarily signify nothing more than this; and here also they are not used in any other sense. What confusion arises when some other meaning is put into them will be seen below." [2]

It is impossible to over-emphasise the importance of this distinction between materialist and idealist philosophy. All consistent thinkers belonging to either "camp" have recognised it. Sometimes it figures under the name "naturalism versus supernaturalism." Sometimes the opposites are called "realism" and "idealism." But (apart from misunderstandings which will be considered in Chapter VIII) the distinction is always between the kind of philosophy which glorifies mind, ideas, spirit—whether human or "divine"—exalting them above mere matter and external conditions (as *idealist* philosophy does), and that other kind of philosophy which sees these intellectual processes as secondary and dependent, as only arising at a given stage in the evolution of the material universe (which is the view of the *materialist* philosophy).

It will be understood that this philosophical use of the terms "idealism" and "materialism" is quite different from their customary colloquial use. A philosophical idealist may be—and frequently is—a "gross materialist" in the ordinary sense. But there is nothing to prevent a philosophical materialist holding political ideals, provided these are scientifically grounded. It is against this confusion that Engels warns us in the above passage.

One might have hoped that it would have been common ground to all would-be "Marxists" by now. But unfortunately certain representatives of what T. A. Jackson calls the "Anglo-American school of Marxism" have fallen into this elementary trap. See for example Casey's *Method in Thinking* (p. 125), also the remarkable passage in the same book which concludes (p. 153) by advising the proletariat in some cases to foster idealism.*

---

* Later in Chapters VII and VIII we shall see something of Casey's dialectics. Meanwhile it is amusing to note the same Comrade Casey who is

Later on we will meet with attempts to "transcend" these two basic philosophies, attempts to build a neutral philosophy which shall be neither materialism nor idealism. But all such attempts get shipwrecked against reality. We will find that they are as impossible as the famous "non-party" attitude in politics.

The Logical Roots of Idealism

Idealist philosophy may have its roots in the theological conception of the world. But to-day it is generally supported by arguments of a logico-metaphysical character. Its advocates attempt to show that the very nature of human knowledge leads to idealist conclusions. Materialism, with its "dogmatic" belief in the outer world, becomes with these advocates a mere obstinate prejudice which will not stand the test of critical thinking. Let us take a look at the sort of arguments that are produced in favour of his idealist philosophy.

If we open almost any modern popular book on philosophy we will find that the argument starts off by creating a certain atmosphere of *doubt*.*

Thus Joad, in his *Guide to Philosophy*, begins with the question, "What do we know of the outside world?" He then proceeds to examine a number of statements embodying the "common-sense" view of the world, and concludes that ". . . it is reasonably certain that in the form in which we have just stated them, none of them is true." A similar path is followed by Bertrand Russell in many of his writings. We will take the form he gives the argument in his *Problems of Philosophy*.

---

guilty of the elementary blunder here referred to, is so kind as to point out the "bad dialectics" and "muddled thinking" in Lenin and to show him how —via Dietzgen through Casey—his mistakes may be corrected!

* This "method of systematic doubt" was introduced into modern philosophy by the Frenchman Descartes, whose philosophical starting-point was "I think, therefore I am."

In this book Russell starts off by asking if there is "any knowledge in the world that is so certain that no reasonable man could doubt it?" To the philosopher in his study (who assumes, by the way, that he has an unquestioned title to "reasonableness") there seems very little of such knowledge indeed. This table, of whose "solid reality" the ordinary man is so strongly convinced—what do we know about it? True, we experience a certain feeling of "hardness" when we touch it, and we see various coloured images when, as we say, we look at the table from different angles and in different lights. But beyond these feelings and these images, and the fact of their association, the rest is mere inference. Whether or not there may be good reason to believe in the existence of the "real table," or more generally in a material world, all that is primarily "given to us," all that we *know for certain*, are our *sensations* (Russell uses the word "sense-data"). Thus, Russell concludes, "whatever else may be doubtful, some at least of our immediate experiences seem absolutely certain." A "reasonable man" could doubt the existence of a material world as the cause of his sensations, but not the sensations themselves. The point of view arrived at by Russell in this argument is essentially the view of the *sceptical philosophy*, whose most prominent representative, David Hume (1711-76), also regarded his sensations as the most certain form of knowledge, and declared it impossible to decide "whether they arise immediately from the object, or are produced by the creative power of the mind, or are derived from the author of our being." Much the same view was held by nineteenth-century *agnosticism*, and in Chapter VIII we will examine in more detail its twentieth-century form. For the present we will merely observe that it is a very half-hearted and inconsistent halting-place in an argument, which pursued logically leads to unqualified idealism.

Bishop Berkeley (1685-1753), who came before Hume,

used the sceptical arguments we have indicated, not merely as reasons for doubting the existence of a material world, but as proof positive that all reality is somehow "mental." With Berkeley this view, which is full-blown philosophical idealism, takes the more definite shape that so-called material objects are really thoughts in the mind of the Creator. It is not surprising that Berkeley was able to use his philosophy to give a "reasoned defence" of Christianity, which earned him his bishopric. But there is no reason to stop the argument at the point where the open idealists leave off. We can follow still further along this "path of descent into hell," and passing beyond the position of sceptical and idealist philosophy reach *solipsism*—the "skeleton in the cupboard" of idealist philosophy. Solipsism is the view that nothing exists except "my" sensations, that all the objects of the world, including other people are "but complexes of sensations" (and *my* sensations at that!).

Idealist philosophers (including Russell, in his above-mentioned book) are always stumbling over this difficulty, and then running away from it as hard as they can. It must be admitted that *starting* from a belief in nothing except "my" sensations it is very hard to "prove" the existence of anything else. But the true position is even worse than we have indicated. We may doubt the accuracy of our memories, even the continuity of thought required to complete a sentence, and thus arrive at a "philosophy" called "solipsism of the present moment." Needless to say its adherents are not to be found outside lunatic asylums!

This is a strange path that we have followed. We started with the philosopher in his study, consumed with doubt in the real existence of his writing table. We next found ourselves in the company of a philosophising bishop, who rejected the alleged "dogma" of matter in order to substitute the very real dogmas of religion. And we ended amid the ravings of an insane asylum. This line of argument which starts with "philosophical doubt" is truly self-destructive. Yet it is recommended to us as the only "strictly scientific" method, which starts "right at the beginning" and makes "no arbitrary assumptions." Have we then really no alternative?

The Materialist Answer to Idealism

If we are to avoid these self-destructive conclusions we must abandon completely the line of argument which led to them. We must reject that innocent-looking philosophical doubt, which pretends to start with the minimum of assumptions, but really denies the existing world in order to replace it by arbitrary fantasies of the philosopher. We must adopt in our reasoning that same *materialist* standpoint which we all adopt in practice in our daily lives, a standpoint which was thus expressed by Marx and Engels in one of their earliest works:

> "The premises from which we begin are not arbitrary ones, not dogmas, but are real premises from which abstraction can only be made in the imagination. They are the real individuals, their activity and the material conditions under which they live, both those which they find already existing and those produced by their activity. These premises can thus be verified in a purely empirical way." [3]

"Real premises from which abstraction can only be made in imagination," here we have the essential materialist critique of idealism, the refusal to make an unreal abstraction from what is actually "given us," and to substitute the shadowy "ideas" and "sense-data" of the philosopher. To those idealists who would ask us, how can you prove the existence of a material world? we would reply, how can you *doubt* it? * Since we

* In the assertion "I," "my," or "mine" our own material existence is presupposed. In our own existence are presupposed all the requisites for that existence including the material universe. Thus if the idealist starts with "I" or "my" sensations he tacitly concedes the material universe he proceeds to juggle into non-existence.

must judge idealist philosophers as we do political parties, by their *actions* and not by their *words*, we conclude that idealists cannot in practice disbelieve in a material world, which does not depend for its existence on their sensations. Among the philosophers even Hume admitted that it was impossible to carry sceptical philosophy outside the study.

The materialist standpoint has been thus put by Levy in a recent book:

> "The universe is our datum, it is given, it exists, it is the every-day world of common sense and common experience. It is a world of process. Mankind is just such a changing feature, a compound and indissoluble part of it, and yet so definitely differentiated from the whole that it is easily induced to isolate itself in thought as if it were an independent thing; and therein as we have seen, lies a danger." [4]

This materialist standpoint is the true alternative to idealist scepticism. Unlike the latter it is not self-destructive. Nor is it "uncritical." It is the practical standpoint on which natural science has worked from the earliest times. And as we have already indicated, and will verify in detail when we come to deal with "empirical matter," this standpoint is just as essential for the science of society.

The Social Roots of Idealism and Materialism

Idealism and materialism are two ways of looking at the world. But the struggle between them is no mere struggle of abstract principles. It is essentially a reflection of the contradictions and conflicts in modern class-divided society. That is why the founders of Marxism (and later on Lenin) paid such great attention to it.

Idealist philosophy leads to a sceptical attitude towards science, to "masked" theological conceptions (if not to open supernaturalism), and to the obscurantist misdescription of existing human relationships. It thus becomes a useful buttress of the capitalist order.

Materialist philosophy, on the other hand, is challenging, critical, revolutionary. It makes clear the actual nature of human relationships, and it demands that human action be based upon scientific study of the real world instead of upon pleasant, mental fantasies. It was their thoroughgoing materialist outlook that enabled Marx and Engels to make a science of Socialism.*

> "If materialism in general explains consciousness as the outcome of existence, and not conversely, then materialism as applied to the social life of mankind must explain *social* consciousness as the outcome of *social* existence." [5]

We have here in fact the opposition between the points of view of Scientific and of Utopian Socialism already noted, and we see that this opposition is merely a special case of the general opposition between materialist and idealist philosophy. In view of the bourgeois connections of idealist philosophy to-day, it is not surprising that so many Utopians (e.g. J. R. MacDonald) have come to a bad end! †

In Chapter VIII we will examine more fully the development of this philosophical conflict in the conditions of the modern class struggle. Here we have just gone into sufficient detail to characterise materialism and idealism very briefly, and to explain why the outlook of the militant proletariat must be *materialist*. In the next chapter we will review the history of materialism, and will show why the proletarian outlook must also be *dialectical*.

---

* All idealism is forced to deny the bare possibility of a science of human society.

† Note also the pragmatist solipsist support given to Trotsky.

II. MATERIALISM: MECHANICAL
AND DIALECTICAL

My dialectic method is not only different from the Hegelian, but is its direct opposite.[1] MARX.

Early Materialism

"What is the primary stuff of the Universe?" The earliest known school of Greek philosophers, the Milesians, were engaged in finding a thoroughly materialist answer to this question. While Thales believed this primary substance to be water, his pupil Anaximander is reported to have maintained that, "It is neither water nor any other of the so-called elements, but a substance different from them which is infinite, from which arise all the heavens and the worlds within them." * This substance he held to be eternal and ageless and said that it "encompasses all the worlds." "And besides this, there was an eternal motion, in which was brought about the origin of the worlds."

Here in the case of Anaximander we can see how powerfully the materialist world outlook stimulates scientific speculation. He was the first to maintain that the earth swings freely in space without need of support. Still more remarkable was his anticipation of the modern theory of evolution. Fragments of his teachings have been preserved which leave no doubt that Anaximander believed (1) that all life originated from the sea, and (2) that man arose from fish life by some process of adaptation. Of course, these were only "speculations." The necessary groundwork of detailed scientific investigation had not yet been laid. But they show how already at this very early

* These quotations are taken from Burnett's *Early Greek Philosophy*.

date the materialist outlook pointed the way to scientific advance.

The "Milesian School" of philosophy is named after the important Greek town of Miletus which gave birth to it. In George Henry Lewes' *History of Philosophy* we are told that "Miletus was one of the most flourishing Greek colonies—its commerce by sea and land was immense. Its political constitution afforded opportunity for individual activity."

Here then we meet those social conditions which were often in later times to prove favourable to the materialist world outlook. In general, materialism has been the banner of progressive classes throughout history, whether the ancient commercial classes, the bourgeoisie in its revolutionary period, or the modern proletariat.

Later Greek philosophy developed more on idealist lines (in Chapter VI we will consider some important aspects of this development). But great materialist thinkers also appeared. Such were Leucippus and Democritus, originators of the atomic conception of matter, who did much to inspire scientific thought at a later time. There were also thinkers like Aristotle, the basic content of whose teaching is materialistic.

When the Greek world decayed and political reaction triumphed materialist philosophy disappeared, to give place to the most reactionary varieties of mysticism and supernaturalism.

Mechanical Materialism

The early Greek materialists made brilliant guesses about the nature of things. Their work is a kind of "scientific poetry." But it was not founded on a really scientific method, on a detailed scientific study of the world. In Greek society, based as it was primarily on land-cultivation by slaves, the social motives for such a development of science were lacking. These motives first became powerful with the growth of commodity production in Europe, particularly from the sixteenth century onwards. The bourgeoisie needed scientific, materialist thinking for two reasons. In the first place it required to develop natural science, especially mechanics, for the sake of its industrial applications. But, secondly, it was necessary to challenge the intellectual stranglehold of the Papal Church, and its Royalist-absolute offshoots, which were the main props of the feudal order.

In Great Britain, one of the first countries in which feudalism was undermined, there appeared a crop of materialist philosophers (including Bacon, Locke and Hobbes as outstanding figures in the seventeenth century) leading Marx to say that "Materialism is the natural-born son of Great Britain." [2] Unfortunately, when the British bourgeoisie lost the revolutionary ardour of its youth and became respectably conservative, this same materialist philosophy was later treated as an illegitimate son!

The materialism that grew up in this period was profoundly affected by the development of science. The outstanding achievement of the first phase in the development of modern science (from the sixteenth to the eighteenth century) was Mechanics. This was developed by Newton to a high stage of perfection, and became for some time a model to all sciences of what an "exact science" should be. Most of physics was in a much more primitive state (indeed it required the prior development of mechanics) and still less was known of chemistry or biology. Thus mechanics dominated science and the philosophy that arose from it may be termed mechanical materialism.

Mechanical Materialism looked upon the world as on some very complicated machine, which has been wound up some time and then set going according to fixed, unalterable laws to all eternity. There was no room in such a scheme for evolution or any sort of real change. This mode of thinking was "metaphysical" (in the sense used by Hegel and later by Marxists). That is to say, it saw everything in terms of hard and fast absolutes, polar opposites which mutually excluded each other, and for it the rigid distinctions of formal logic represented the final law. The logic of this mode of thinking will be specially examined in Chapter V.

Meanwhile as an illustration of mechanical materialism, we may take the great French materialist D'Holbach, who concluded some scientific speculations with these words: "If one were to reject all the previous conjectures, if one were to pretend that nature acts through a certain sum of unchangeable and general laws: if one were to believe that man, the quadruped, fish, insects, plants, etc., have always existed and will for ever remain as they are: if one were to insist that the stars would shine in the firmament for all eternity, we should not object." [3]

D'Holbach is here speaking for the whole school of French materialists that prepared men's minds in the eighteenth century for the coming revolution. The limitations of their standpoint were above all revealed whenever they came to deal with human society. They could reject such things as despotism and religion as "bad"—even the whole middle ages could be dismissed as a "bad thing," rather in the spirit of that well-known history book *1066 And All That!* But they were powerless to explain the historical events they condemned. Such an explanation was made impossible by the basic defect of their philosophy, its failure to understand development.

Dialectical Idealism and its Materialist Inversion

The defects of mechanical materialism led to an idealist reaction which grew in intensity as the bourgeoisie everywhere shrank back from a truly revolutionary role.* In the eighteenth century the materialist philosophers considered that they had destroyed idealism. But:

> "During the first four decades of the nineteenth century nobody would hear a word of materialism, which, in its turn, was considered to be dead and buried. The materialist doctrine appeared for the whole philosophical and literary world as it appeared to Goethe, as 'grey,' 'gloomy' and 'dead': 'People shuddered before it as before a spectre' (Goethe). Speculative philosophy was confident in its turn that its rival was forever defeated" (Plekhanov).[4]

The leaders in this idealist revolt were the classical German philosophers, especially Kant and Hegel, who criticised exhaustively the weak points of eighteenth-century materialism, its "hard and fast metaphysical way of thinking" and developed in opposition to this a dialectical philosophy which "studied things in their development, in their arising and dying away" (Plekhanov).[5] Dialectical thinking became essential in science once the narrow boundaries of mechanics were crossed, and in particular as soon as such fundamental facts as the evolution of the species were recognised (in the next chapter the new facts which were then revolutionising science and compelling it to be dialectical will be considered).

But such a dialectical outlook was most of all important for an understanding of history and social development. Here it is the great service of Hegel to have conceived history as exhibiting a process of development, instead of as a "chapter of accidents" where everything is determined by the arbitrary caprices of "great men" (a view then dominant and often to be found among bourgeois historians to-day—see Chapter IV).

The basic defect of all idealist philosophy, its arbitrary

---

* Mechanical materialism had its reactionary side in its limitation of the role of social revolution to *restoring* the "natural order" which had become perverted by kings and priests.

a priori nature, prevented the rational use of the dialectical method developed by Hegel. Instead of studying the laws of development of the real world by the methods of science, an attempt was made to deduce these laws from a study of ideas and concepts (which were themselves but pictures, more or less accurate) of the world.

According to Hegel, dialectics is the self-development of the concept. "The absolute concept does not only exist—*where* unknown—from eternity, it is also the actual living soul of the whole existing world" (Engels).[6] Again:

"According to Hegel, therefore, the dialectical development apparent in nature and history, i.e. the causal interconnection of the progressive movement from the lower to the higher, which asserts itself through all zig-zag movements and temporary set-backs, is only a miserable copy of the self-movement of the concept going on from eternity, no one knows where, but at all events independently of any thinking human brain" (Engels).[7]

It was against this substitution of the mystical "concept" for material reality that Marx and Engels revolted when they turned the dialectic of Hegel "upon its head"—"or, rather, [was] turned off its head, on which it was standing before, and placed upon its feet again" (Engels).[8]

Thus understood, dialectics was no longer a "holy mystery" but simply "reduced itself to the science of the general laws of motion—both of the external world and of human thought." [9]

Materialism came into its own again, but no longer the mechanist materialism of the past, for dialectical materialism took over from the intervening period of idealist philosophy the real achievement of this philosophy—its dialectic method—and applied this with a really scientific, materialist attitude to reality.

Dialectical materialism appears at first sight to be a return to the original Greek view of the world from which philosophy started. And indeed, like this Greek materialism, it sees the world as a single interconnected whole in endless motion, a point of view which was lost when the development of the special sciences broke up this single picture of the world. But we must not forget that it stands on a very different basis from the naïve materialism of the Greeks. It rests on "the whole thought content of two thousand years of development of philosophy and natural science, as well as of the historical development of these two thousand years." [10] If therefore it is a return to the old, it is a return "on a higher level" and is an example of that dialectical form of development known as "the negation of the negation" which we are soon to investigate.

Dialectical Materialism as the Philosophy of the Proletariat

The philosophy of dialectical materialism whose evolution we have just described, was first championed by Marx and Engels as representatives of the revolutionary workers' movement. Bourgeois Nature-Materialists of which there are a few modern representatives, besides others who continue the tradition of the eighteenth-century materialists, have never been able to rise above the narrow, mechanist limitations of the old materialism.

Contemporary idealism always catches on to this weakness, and is never tired of vanquishing its old enemy, mechanical materialism, afresh. Here is a typical example of such a "refutation" (from Joad's *Meaning of Life*):

> "Thus Materialism explains everything in terms of different arrangements and constructions of bits of matter. Little bits of matter wandering aimlessly in space have produced our hopes and fears, the scent of the rose, the colour of the sunset, and the mystic's experience of God."

(Note the high moral affectation of this effusion and its deliberate invitation to reactionary supernaturalism!)

It is clear that such a refutation does not apply to dialectical materialism, which is far from denying the specific nature of the qualities that appear in the successive stages of material evolution (see Chapter III). Nor is dialectical materialism perturbed by the "mystics' experience of God." On the contrary —and here lies its superiority over the old materialism—it understands the social roots of such phenomena, and is even able to explain what Mr. Joad is doing in such strange company!

It is no accident that consistent representatives of dialectical materialism are only to be found in the ranks of the workers' movement. The basic principle of this philosophy, the unity of theory and practice (which, properly understood, contains both its dialectical and materialist aspects) requires that this should be so. But for those who are still under the influence of bourgeois, mechanistic thinking, one of whose inherent vices is the separation of theory from practice, this is a hard saying. As this point of view is expressly challenged in a recently published *Introduction to Dialectical Materialism* by E. Conze, it is necessary to say something more about it.

Dr. Conze, who, by the way, uses the name "Dialectical Materialism" in his title, presumably to attract readers, is extremely dissatisfied with this name. It appears that it "has all the disadvantages that a name can possibly have. It is cumbersome and unwieldly, unintelligible to the average person and extremely vague to the expert." Dr. Conze therefore decides to dispense with this name, and explains that "since the Marxist scientific method is the correct and only scientific one, and since it is, as we shall see, not restricted to Marxists, we will simply speak of 'scientific method' instead of 'dialectical materialism.' " Dr. Conze then goes on to point out that the stupidity of the Communists who "honestly believe that the scientific method in the Marxist sense can be clearly understood only by such persons as prove to be clear-minded enough to join the Communist parties—if only temporarily."

All this is very clear—but we confess to a few doubts. In the first place, Conze's argument is rooted in the separation of theory from practice already noted. It introduces the idea of the non-Marxist (perhaps anti-Marxist) using the Marxist scientific method. Conze would perhaps reply that this might be possible for a natural scientist in his own restricted field. But even here we have enough examples—some of which were noted by Engels in his time, but we have had more, and worse since—of scientists getting hopelessly confused in their own specialties, precisely because of the metaphysical, idealist limitations of bourgeois thought. And even where this is not the case, the fact remains of fundamental importance, that no thinking within one compartment however dialectical, makes the general outlook of the scientist dialectical materialism.

Conze's terminology does not "clear up things." Under cover of doing away with unintelligible terms, it obliterates the distinction between what commonly passes for "scientific method" (an eclectic hodge-podge of bourgeois metaphysics) and the Marxist scientific method. It covers up the whole historical evolution of dialectical materialism (of which there is not a mention anywhere in the book).

Indeed, this *Introduction to Dialectical Materialism* does not once explain the term "materialism" nor refer to the age-long struggle around what Engels called "the basic question of philosophy"! We are left in doubt of Conze's position on this issue. Probably (like past revisers and "improvers" of Marxism) he would regard it as an "antiquated" issue, not worth troubling about. But we have seen that it is around this issue that the class fronts in modern philosophy are mainly formed. So Conze's "little omission" succeeds in robbing revolutionary

Marxism of its class content, in castrating it and converting it into a harmless plaything.

Conze does not even think it necessary to settle accounts with Marx and Engels on these matters. If Marx used the term "dialectical materialism" to describe his standpoint, that merely proves he has a "passion for clumsy and far-fetched terms." This is certainly an easy method of dealing with one's predecessors and a fine example of "scientific method"! (though not of the Marxist scientific method). But perhaps it is explainable if we adopt the point of view of those stupid Communists about the unity of theory and practice, and if we remember that Conze is not now in the ranks of the revolutionary movement. How far away he stands from those ranks we will see in Chapter VI—on *Dialectics and Sophistry*.

III. THE GENERAL NATURE
OF DIALECTICS

The general nature of Dialectics as the science of connections, to be developed in contrast to Metaphysics.[1] ENGELS.

Dialectics and Natural Science

We have shown how dialectical materialism arose as a philosophy that studies the world as a whole in its process of development, in contrast to the old materialism, based on Newtonian Mechanics and the so-called "organic" sciences (sciences of life forms), which had not progressed beyond the stage of mere classification. We have also seen that the primary urge to the dialectical revolution in philosophy came from the need to understand human history.

But in the nineteenth century big advances were made in natural science which proved that here also dialectical interconnection and development were everywhere to be found. Engels mentions three major discoveries as being of decisive importance for changing the outlook of natural science.

"The first was the proof of the transformation of energy.... All the innumerable operative causes in nature, which until then had led a mysterious, inexplicable existence as so-called 'forces'—mechanical force, heat, radiation (light and radiant heat), electricity, magnetism, the force of chemical combination and dissociation—are now proved to be special forms, modes of existence of one and the same energy, i.e., motion. The unity of all motion in nature is no longer a philosophical assertion but a fact of natural science."

"The second—chronologically earlier—discovery was that of the organic cell by Schwann and Schleiden—of the cell as the unit, out of the multiplication and differentiation of which all organisms, except the very lowest, arise and develop."

"But an essential gap still remained. If all multicellular organisms—plants as well as animals, including man—grow from a
single cell according to the law of cell-division, whence, then,
comes the infinite variety of these organisms? This question was
answered by the third great discovery, the theory of evolution,
which was first presented in connected form and substantiated by
Darwin." [2]

These discoveries introduced dialectics into science because
they did away with the absolute boundaries formerly thought
to exist between the different "forces" of nature, and because
everywhere they showed transformation, evolution, growth—in
a word, motion—to be the fundamental aspect of nature, which
must be appealed to in order to explain the existing properties
of "things." But it did not follow that scientists became thereby
conscious or consistent dialecticians. On the contrary, there followed an epoch of theoretical confusion, in which fragments
of the old conception of the world were mixed up with the
new, a muddle which could only be fully cleared up by consciously adopting the viewpoint of dialectical materialism.

The Laws of Dialectical Process

In order to help this process of dialectically mastering the
new results of the special sciences, and so bring them into a
unified whole, Engels made a special study of nineteenth-
century natural science. The results of this study are embodied
partly in his famous *Anti-Dühring*, but still more in that rich
storehouse of thought, the incompleted manuscript of *Natur-
Dialektik* (i.e. *Dialectics of Nature*).

This study convinced Engels:

"In detail—of which in general I was not in doubt—that amid
the welter of innumerable changes taking place in nature, the
same dialectical laws of motion are in operation as those which
in history govern the apparent fortuitousness of events; the same
laws as those which similarly form the thread running through

the history of the development of human thought and gradually rise to consciousness in the mind of man; the laws which Hegel first developed in an all-embracing but mystical form, and which we made it our aim to strip of this mystic form and to bring clearly before the mind in their complete simplicity and universality." [3]

The "dialectical laws of motion" here referred to by Engels are simply the most general features of *process, change, development,* common to all "fields" which make up the subject matter of the special sciences. Just because these different "fields," while clearly distinguishable, are also and at the same time no more than particular aspects of one single *world process,* we should expect to find such common features. These dialectical laws are of course the most general laws possible. In what follows we will see how they provide a method applicable to each of the special sciences.

In spite of his idealistic approach Hegel gave many striking illustrations of dialectics. He was the first to give the "classical" formulation of these laws as:

(1) The law of the transformation of quantity into quality, and *vice-versa.*

(2) The law of the unity (interpenetration, identity) of opposites.

(3) The law of the negation of the negation.

Engels adopted this formulation in his researches, while Marx often refers to these laws in his writings. We will explain and illustrate these laws by means of examples, before passing on to the more *systematic* and *unified* treatment which was given by Lenin.

The Law of the Transformation of Quantity into Quality and Vice-Versa

This law is essential for an understanding of the rise of *new* qualities, and also for understanding the quantitative effects which may follow the appearance of such new qualities. It is one of the fundamental superiorities of dialectical over mechanical materialism that the former understands how new qualities can arise at certain nodal * points of quantitative change— points where the change in quantity literally *becomes* qualitative change.

The simplest (and classical) example is the *change of state* of a substance, e.g. when a liquid becomes a gas (through boiling) or a solid (through freezing). Everyone knows that in such a case, gradual increase or decrease of temperature produces no departure from the quality of liquidity until suddenly a point is reached where a complete transformation is effected. The liquid (as Hegel says) does not gradually become more and more gelatinous and semi-solid. It leaps at one bound from the liquid state to the solid. The reader who is acquainted with elementary physics and chemistry will be able to find dozens of more "sophisticated" examples of this kind. Especially in chemistry does everything depend on the number and kind of atoms in the molecule, leading Engels to say that "chemistry can be described as the science of the qualitative changes in bodies as the result of changed quantitative composition." [4]

Examples of this law in the science of human society are just as numerous, and of even more importance, owing to the fact that this is no "exact science" in which changes can be quantitatively predicted. The social revolution itself is just such a "jump," where accumulated quantitative alterations pass into qualitative change. In the next chapter we will see how this conception of change by means of *revolutionary leaps* distinguishes the Marxist from the Fabian or "gradualist" view of social evolution. Marx's great work *Capital* is full of examples

* A "node" is the term used by Hegel to denote the points beyond which a thing cannot vary while remaining the same thing. On passing the "nodal" line it becomes something else, or "other."

of this dialectical law (specially Part IV, *Production of Relative Surplus Value,* which treats of the different *stages* in the development of modern large-scale industry). On the other hand when a qualitative change has taken place, such as the coming into existence of large-scale capitalist industry, this is in itself productive of the greatest quantitative changes in many fields (e.g. increase in political activity of the masses, their state of education, etc.).

In the practical work of a revolutionary movement examples are just as frequent. Take for instance the growth and development of the revolutionary party. This does not proceed smoothly and evenly, but as everyone knows in an extremely jerky manner. This does not mean that slow quantitative changes are not taking place here all the time, but their full effect only becomes apparent when they have sufficiently accumulated to force a complete "change in the political situation," locally or nationally.*

In the human thought-process this law is exemplified by any case of the emergence (whether in the consciousness of the individual or of society) of a *new* idea or theory. As illustrations we may take the philosophical tendencies we have studied, but examples may equally be drawn from such wide-apart fields as scientific theory and musical idiom.

The Law of the Unity of Opposites

The second dialectical law, that of "the unity, interpenetration or identity of opposites" (as the case may be) asserts the essentially *contradictory* character of reality—and at the same time asserts that these "opposites" which are everywhere to be found do not remain in stark, metaphysical opposition, but also

---

* It is important to remember that dialectical materialism does not deny gradualism in social development. It is not a question of *either* gradualism or non-gradualism. What has to be grasped is *both* in conjunction, the qualitative leap in the quantitative series.

exist in unity. This law was known to the early Greeks. It was classically expressed by Hegel over a hundred years ago:

"Positive and negative are supposed to express an absolute difference. The two however are at bottom the same; the name of either might be transformed to the other. Thus, for example, debts and assets are not two particular, self-subsisting species of property. What is negative to the debtor is positive to the creditor. A way to the East is also a way to the West. Positive and negative are therefore intrinsically conditioned by one another, and are only in relation to each other. The North Pole of the magnet cannot be without the South Pole and *vice-versa*. If we cut a magnet in two, we have not a North Pole in one piece and a South Pole in the other. Similarly, in electricity, the positive and the negative are not two diverse and independent fluids. In opposition the difference is not confronted by *any* other, but by *its* other." [5]

The lapse of a century has only served to emphasise this universal co-existence of opposites noted by Hegel. As Bernal has stated:

"The history of the physical sciences in the nineteenth and twentieth centuries shows a steady drift away from the mechanical views of Newton into a set of irreducible dialectical opposites such as—wave and particle, matter and energy, statistical and determinate, aggregating and segregating processes." [6]

The importance of understanding this contradictory character of things, is that it gives the clue to the *inner* process of their development, which takes place through the conflict of these opposites. That is why Lenin called contradiction "the salt of dialectics" [7] and stated that "the division of the one and the cognition of its contradictory parts is the *essence* of dialectics." [8]

In the next chapter we will see how Marxism explained the evolution of human society by unearthing the fundamental contradiction which was the driving force of that evolution.

Meanwhile as an illustration of contradictions (which are not just "flat" contradictions) in the realm of thought, we may consider the origin of the word "dialectic" in its present sense. This has been explained as derived by Hegel from the same root as "dialogue"—the idea being that the conflict of opposites, which leads to the dialectical movement in general, is essentially similar to that clash of opinions, which "in the course of a lively and fruitful conversation" [9] leads to the emergence of some new point of view.

In interpreting and applying this dialectical law of the unity of opposites we must beware of letting the "unity" swallow up the fundamental "opposition." As we will see, with the help of an "awful" example, in Chapter VI, the *unity* exists only from a relative, restricted standpoint—the temporary "here and now." But from the standpoint of the developing universe as a whole, what is vital is not this temporary "here and now" but rather the motion and change which follows from the *conflict* of the opposite.

The Law of the Negation of the Negation

This law states one of the most characteristic features of evolutionary process in all fields—that development takes place in a kind of spiral, one change negating a given state of affairs and a succeeding change, which negated the first, re-establishing (in a more developed form, or "on a higher plane" as it is often expressed) some essential feature of the original state of affairs.

In the last chapter we considered an example of this law in the history of human thought—the development of modern dialectical materialism by means of a negation of that mechanical materialism which was itself a negation of the original "naïve" materialist conception of the world.

This law of dialectical process is like the others in that it cannot be arbitrarily "foisted" upon Nature or history. It cannot be used as a substitute for empirical facts, or used to "predict" things without a concrete study of the facts in question (cf. Chapters V and VI). Marx and Engels were very emphatic about this. But despite their explicit statements to the contrary, the accusation that they *did* so use dialectics (in an *idealist* way) is one of the commonest reproaches levelled against Marxism—ever since a certain Dr. Dühring, in the year 1875, discovered that Marx had proved the inevitability of the proletarian revolution mystically, by means of the law of the negation of the negation. Since essentially the same "discovery" has been made in our up-to-date English world over half a century later by two English publishers (B. Russell and E. Carritt) it will be well to reproduce the gist of Engels' reply to Dühring.

At the end of the chapter of *Capital* entitled *Historical Tendency of Capitalist Accumulation,* in which the early history of capitalism is reviewed, Marx sums up his conclusion in these words:

> "The capitalist mode of appropriation, the result of the capitalist mode of production, produces capitalist private property. This is the first negation of individual private property, as founded on the labour of the proprietor. But capitalist production begets, with the inexorability of a law of Nature, its own negation. It is the negation of negation." [10]

This does not re-establish private property for the producer, but gives him individual property based on the acquisitions of the capitalist era, i.e. on co-operation and the possession in common of the land and of the "means of production." If read by itself, i.e. in false undialectical isolation from the rest of the book, this passage might conceivably be misunderstood in the way indicated. But coming at the conclusion of a vast detailed study of the workings of capitalism, in a section where it is shown that the very development of capitalism of necessity *intensifies* the proletarian struggle against it, there can be no excuse except the incurable blindness of bourgeois thinkers, for such misrepresentation. Rather must we agree with Engels when he says:

> "Marx merely shows from history, and in this passage states in a summarised form, that just as the former petty industry necessarily, through its own development, created the conditions of its own annihilation, i.e., of the expropriation of the small proprietors, so now the capitalist mode of production has likewise itself created the material conditions which will annihilate it. The process is an historical one, and if it is at the same time a dialectical process, this is not Marx's fault, however annoying it may be for Herr Dühring." [11]

Dialectics as a Method

The account of the dialectical laws just given may seem somewhat arbitrary and disjointed. That is because, for the purposes of easy explanation, we have singled out certain particular aspects of dialectical process (the most important aspects undoubtedly) and illustrated these by examples drawn from diverse fields. But in doing this we have not brought out with sufficient clearness the essential unity of these different aspects of dialectics. Our treatment has not itself been sufficiently dialectical.

This weakness we will attempt to remedy by explaining the very systematic dialectical "methodology" which was given by Lenin in his *Notes on Hegel's Logic*. In these *Notes* Lenin writes that: "Dialectics may be briefly defined as the theory of the unity of opposites. That covers the kernel of dialectics but needs explanation and development." [12] This "explanation and development" he proceeds to give in some sixteen points, whose internal movement and life correspond to the objective dialectic of the world that they reflect. We will reproduce these points together with some brief explanations.

All thinking has to start by abstracting or "isolating" certain features of the world process, by concentrating on these to the exclusion of others. Thinking has to start with *objects, things.* Therefore the first requirement of dialectical thinking is, very simply, to view things as they actually are in their separation—or Lenin's point (1) "*Objectivity* of observation (not examples, not unrepresentative forms, but the thing itself)."

But this first step, breaking up the dialectic of reality, has to be completed by a further step reforming that dialectic.

> "If the universe is an inter-related changing process, we recognise it in parts by separating out, in thought, certain partial processes—aspects such, for example, as society, the means of production, changing objects, words. These we will call Isolates. An isolate is something that has been dragged from its environment in space, time, and matter. By itself, therefore, it is a fiction, for dialectically nothing can be free of environment; but it is a real fiction in the sense that it really does have an objective existence. The first step in the study of the dialectic is to chip out its isolates, to study them, and then *to remake the dialectic by seeing them again in their environment*" (Levy; our italics, D. G.).[13]

Only by taking this second step of *remaking* the dialectic (which is a true "negation of the negation") can we overcome metaphysical isolation and one-sidedness, can we see the world again in its interconnections and movement. This second step is Lenin's point (2) that we must consider "the totality of the manifold *relations* of each thing to others."

Everything is not only part of the great world process but is itself essentially a process. Its "nature" cannot be understood apart from the form of change it undergoes, that is inherent in it. We must therefore consider point (3) "the *development* of the thing or the phenomenon, its own movement, its own life."

But this development is not something that proceeds in an automatic fashion, without cause, "mystically." Development is always the result of internal conflict as well as of external relations, themselves including conflict. It can only be explained and rationally grasped to the extent that the internal contradictions of the thing have been investigated. Hence Lenin's point (4) that we must search for "the inner contradictory *tendencies* (*and sides*) in the thing," and must see point (5) "the thing (appearance, etc.) as the sum and *unity of opposites*"; we must also examine point (6) "the *struggle* or unfolding of these opposites, that which conflicts with these strivings, etc."

Every "thing" is itself vastly complicated, made up of innumerable sides and aspects, related in various ways to every other thing. It can only be understood by the combined process of splitting up into these parts (analysis) and seeing them in their inter-relation (synthesis). This process is inexhaustible in the wealth of aspects revealed by each successive stage of analysis. These considerations are more precisely indicated in Lenin's points 7-12 which run as follows:

(7) Union of *analysis* and *synthesis*, the splitting into the separate parts and the totality, summation of these parts together.

(8) The *relations* of each thing (or appearance, etc.) not only manifold, but *general*, *universal*. Each thing (or appearance, process, etc.) is connected with *every other*.

(9) Not only union of opposites, but *transitions* of *each* determination, each quality, each feature, each side, each property in *every* other (into its opposite?).

(10) An *infinite process* of revealing *new* sides, relations, etc.

(11) An infinite process of *deepening the knowledge* of the thing, appearance, process, etc., by man, *from appearance to essence*, and from less deep to deeper essence.

(12) *From co-existence to causality*, and from one form of connection and reciprocal dependence to another deeper and more general.

This struggle of opposites which causes development leads at a certain point to a revolutionary *break*, to the emergence of a new thing (or quality). The main features of this revolutionary jump from one stage to another are described in the remaining points 13-16.

(13) The *repetition* of certain features, properties, etc., of *the lower stage in the higher* and . . .

(14) apparent return to the old (*negation of the negation*).

(15) *The struggle of content with form* and *vice-versa*.

(16) *Passing* of quantity into quality and *vice-versa*.

(15) and (16) are examples of (9).

These sixteen points include those features of the dialectical process already considered. But besides being greatly expanded, they are seen in their real living inter-relationship, they are grasped dialectically.

IV. DIALECTICS OF SOCIETY

Social life is essentially practical. *All mysteries which mislead theory to mysticism find their rational solution in human practice and in the comprehension of this practice.* MARX.[1]

Dialectical Materialism and History

We have approached Dialectical Materialism from what seems to-day the most natural point of view—the point of view of the worker whose practice is already guided by Marxist principles and who wants to grasp more fully the scientific outlook implied by them. But in doing this we have inverted the real order of historical development. Historically, dialectical materialism appeared as the first world outlook to take *human practical activity*, as well as the so-called "external World" as its subject-matter. And for this very reason it gave birth to the science of history, to *Historical Materialism*, more usually known in this country as the *Materialist Conception of History* (the necessary theoretical basis of "scientific socialism").

It is still true that only those who accept the dialectical materialist standpoint treat history as a science (i.e. admit that it points the way to the future, that it is not merely concerned with "writing up" the stale gossip of the past). This is illustrated by a recent book of Bertrand Russell's (*Freedom and Organisation, 1814-1914*) where it is maintained that "history, in short, is not yet a science, and can only be made to seem a science by falsifications and omission" (p. 8).

The refutation of this bourgeois view is simply the continued success of Marxism in predicting the general tendency of world events. Since the world economic crisis, with its accompaniments of the spread of fascism and the practical proof of the economic superiority of the Soviet system—events which can only be understood in terms of Marxism—many bourgeois intellectuals have come to see daylight. It is not impossible that Bertrand Russell will struggle through to clarity, in spite of his *scepticism*. But the bourgeoisie as a class will never be satisfied with this "theoretical" refutation (though it is based on objective social practice). The only refutation that they will find convincing will be the *practical* refutation of their own revolutionary overthrow.

This refusal to treat history as a science is also found in the *Utopian Socialism* already referred to.

The Socialist predecessors of Marx had condemned the evils of capitalism and had painted brilliant pictures of a better social order, but they were unable to *explain* those evils or see the proletariat as the force that would rebuild society. "To all these," as Engels said, "socialism is the expression of absolute truth, reason and justice, and needs only to be discovered to conquer the world by virtue of its own power; as absolute truth is independent of time and space and of the historical development of man, it is a mere accident when and where it is discovered. At the same time, absolute truth, reason and justice are different for the founder of each different school. . . ." [2]

Historically, Marxism arose in opposition to the socialism of the various Utopian sects as the theoretical expression of *actually existing* class struggle. In the words of *The Communist Manifesto*:

"The theoretical conclusions of the Communists are in no way based on ideas or principles that have been invented, or discovered, by this or that would-be universal reformer.

"They merely express, in general terms, actual relations springing from an existing class struggle, from an historical movement going on under our very eyes." [8]

After Marxism had come into existence the Utopian (essentially idealist) view-point lost its historical justification. But it continued to be held by those who wished to oppose the consistent revolutionary standpoint. This *regenerate* Utopianism is still at the bottom of the reformism that has played so disastrous a role in the recent history of the labour movement. As an illustration of the contrast between the Marxist and Utopian points of view we may consider the way in which the social struggle is presented in two books, each of them "classics" but in somewhat different ways.

In the opening passage of *Socialism; Critical and Constructive* by J. R. MacDonald (for thirty years a leading theorist of reformism in Britain) we read: "Two great forces are ever in conflict in the breast of society—habit, the force of stagnation, and reason, the force of change." But on which side is "reason" and which "habit," and who is to be the judge, and how are we to judge when change is proposed from two opposite directions, are surely questions we are entitled to ask.* In actual fact this typical MacDonaldite nebulosity can only serve the purpose of masking the *real struggles* by turning attention to their *ideal reflections* (and reflections in no clear stream but in a very muddy pool indeed, MacDonald's brain). This passage almost cries out for comparison with the challenging opening paragraph of the first section of *The Communist Manifesto:*

"The history of all hitherto existing society [primitive society excepted] is the history of class struggles.

"Freeman and slave, patrician and plebeian, lord and serf, guild-master and journeyman, in a word, oppressor and oppressed stood in constant opposition to one another, carried on an uninterrupted, now hidden, now open fight. . . ." [4]

* MacDonald himself was an example of how "reason" can be used to excuse refusal to change. He blamed the Communists for making a "habit" of changing everything!

What a difference here from the confusing vagueness of a MacDonald! How clearly and sharply this passage stands out, lighting up directly the conflict that has been (at least in historic times) the moving force of social development—*the class struggle*, that struggle whose very existence is to-day denied by the hypocritical bourgeoisie!

The Materialist Conception of History

If we apply our dialectic method to society, if we make this society in process of development our object of consideration, then (as explained in Chapter III) we immediately look for its "inner contradictory tendencies and sides." At first sight we appear to have found the fundamental contradiction in the *class struggle* whose importance is brought out in the above quoted passage from *The Communist Manifesto*.

But with the development of society the "contending classes" have changed. Each social revolution in having solved the issue of one class struggle, has replaced it by new classes and new conflicts. There has also to be taken into account the fact that primitive society knew no classes, and developed notwithstanding, and that there will be no classes in communist society. All this compels us to look deeper for the very source of class conflict.

Marx found the basis of the class struggle to lie in a contradiction between the methods of production (the "material productive forces") and the existing *social relationships* (the "relations of production"). It is this contradiction which during a certain historic period gets expressed in an external *antagonism of classes*. When this is so (for instance under capitalism) one class (e.g. the proletariat) represents the forces of production seeking to expand, and another class (e.g. the bourgeoisie) represents those social relations which are hemming in the productive forces.

But the basic contradiction will continue to exist in classless society, and will cause the progressive development of social relationships as the productive forces themselves develop.

The clearest exposition of this "materialist conception of history" was given by Marx in his preface to *The Critique of Political Economy*, from which we reproduce the most important passage:

"In the social production which men carry on they enter into definite relations that are indispensable and independent of their will; these relations of production correspond to a definite stage of development of their material forces of production. The sum total of these relations of production constitutes the economic structure of society—the real foundation, on which rises a legal and political superstructure and to which correspond definite forms of social consciousness. The mode of production in material life determines the social, political and intellectual life processes in general. It is not the consciousness of men that determines their being, but, on the contrary, their social being that determines their consciousness. At a certain stage of their development, the material forces of production in society come in conflict with the existing relations of production, or—what is but a legal expression for the same thing—with the property relations within which they have been at work before. From forms of development of the forces of production these relations turn into their fetters. Then begins the epoch of social revolution. With the change of the economic foundation the entire immense superstructure is more or less rapidly transformed. In considering such transformations a distinction should always be made between the material transformation of the economic conditions of production which can be determined with the precision of natural science, and the legal, political, religious, æsthetic or philosophic—in short, ideological forms in which men become conscious of this conflict and fight it out. Just as our opinion of an individual is not based on what he thinks of himself, so can we not judge of such a period of transformation by its own consciousness; on the contrary this consciousness must be explained rather from the contradictions of material life, from the existing conflict between the social forces of production and the relations of production. No social order ever disappears before all the productive forces for which there is room in it have been developed; and new higher relations of production never appear before the material conditions of their existence have matured in the womb of the old society itself. Therefore, mankind always sets itself only such tasks as it can solve; since, looking at the matter more closely, we will always find that the task itself arises only when the material conditions necessary for its solution already exist or are at least in the process of formation. In broad outlines we can designate the Asiatic, the ancient, the feudal, and the modern bourgeois modes of production as so many epochs in the progress of the economic formation of society. The bourgeois relations of production are the last antagonistic form of the social process of production—antagonistic not in the sense of individual antagonism, but of one arising from the social conditions of life of the individuals; at the same time the productive forces developing in the womb of bourgeois society create the material conditions for the solution of that antagonism. This social formation constitutes, therefore, the closing chapter of the prehistoric stage of human society." [5]

Some Misunderstandings of the Materialist Conception of History

Superbly clear though the above formulation of the materialist conception of history must seem, and richly though it is supplemented in many writings of Marx and Engels, there is no other side of Marxism that has been more often and more *wilfully* misunderstood. We must therefore clear up a number of points that are most frequently raised in criticism.

In the above quoted passage it will be seen that three *main factors* are distinguished: firstly, the *material productive forces* (also referred to as "the mode of production of the material means of existence"); secondly the *social relations* (or "productive relationships") which would be the immediate relations of producers in classless society but become *class* relations in class society; thirdly, the *ideological* forms of consciousness (juridical, political, religious, æsthetic, philosophic).

This order in which the factors have been given is not arbitrary, but represents the basic materialist element in the Marxist view of society. "It is not the consciousness of men that determines their being, but, on the contrary, their social being that determines their consciousness." The "mode of production" is the ultimate decisive factor influencing the form of society, the conflicts within society, and the types of ideas that become dominant. In this sense the mode of production is often referred to as the "basis," while the social relations and consciousness are called the "superstructure of society."

But it would be wrong to understand this use of the terms *mechanically* in the sense that everything in the "superstructure" is rigidly determined by the "basis." Marx and Engels often protested against this over-simplification (in fact, falsification) of their theories.

"According to the materialist conception of history the determining element in history is *ultimately* the production and reproduction in real life. More than this neither Marx nor I have ever asserted. If therefore somebody twists this into the statement that the economic element is the *only* determining one, he transforms it into a meaningless, abstract and absurd phrase. The economic situation is the basis, but the various elements of the superstructure—political forms of the class struggle and its consequences, constitutions established by the victorious class after a successful battle, etc.—forms of law, and even the reflexes of all these actual struggles in the brains of the combatants: political, legal, philosophical theories, religious ideas and their further development into the systems of dogma—also exercise their influence upon the course of the historic struggles and in many cases preponderate in determining their *form*. There is an interaction of all these elements, in which, amid all the endless *host* of accidents (i.e. of things and events whose interconnection is so remote or so impossible to prove that we can regard it as absent and can neglect it), the economic movement finally asserts itself as necessary. Otherwise the application of the theory to any period of history one chose would be easier than the solution of a simple equation of the first degree." [6]

Closely related to this misconception is the view that Marxism implies a rigid *fatalism*, that the course of history is "destined" inevitably to follow some path quite independently of, and even *in spite of* human wills. Such fatalism is at bottom entirely mystical—only God could "ordain" the world to proceed in this fashion. No view could in fact be more opposed to the spirit of Marxism, which so far from under-rating the importance of human will, seeks rather to explain the *origin* of that will. "Men make their own history," said Marx, "but they do not make it just as they please; they do not make it under circumstances chosen by themselves, but under circumstances directly found, given and transmitted from the past." [7] These circumstances include factors of all three kinds described above, and between them "the mode of production in material life" upon which in the last resort everything else depends, is the finally decisive factor.

Evolution: Marxist and Fabian Conceptions

We have explained how dialectical philosophy brought evolution into vogue, and how later evolutionary views became dominant in science as a result of men like Darwin. While this fact may be recognised to-day there is a widespread tendency to belittle the value of dialectics, and a feeling that evolution in the Darwin-Herbert Spencer sense is after all a more "up-to-date" substitute. This question is closely connected with the opposition of two views of human social development which may be designated briefly as the Fabian view of "the inevitability of gradualness," and the Marxist view of evolution through class struggle with unavoidable revolutionary "jumps."

The former view is naturally popular with bourgeois thinkers. Speaking of the way in which it arose as a reaction from the old metaphysics, Plekhanov says:

"The old metaphysics was stood upon its head. Just as before, phenomena remained separated from one another by an impassable gap. And this metaphysics has become so firmly rooted in the heads of modern evolutionists that there are 'sociologists' to-day who show a complete lack of understanding every time they are compelled in their investigations to deal with revolutions. In their opinion revolution cannot be combined with evolution. *Historia non facit saltus*—history makes no leaps. If in spite of such wisdom revolutions in history nevertheless take place, and even great revolutions, that does not in the least disturb them. They firmly cling to their theory. So much the worse for the revolutions which disturb their calm. They are considered as 'maladies'." [8]

The great weakness of the "gradualist" view is that it is restricted to explaining the growth or decline of something "already there." It is quite unable to explain the origin of anything really *new*. It is here that the supreme importance of dialectics as a method can be seen. By turning attention to the contradictions which give rise to development, and to the revolutionary jumps in that development, dialectics gives an immeasurably superior insight into the *meaning* of the facts discovered by research.

When the Webbs and Hammonds studied the early history of British capitalism they went over essentially the same ground, dealt with the same "raw material" of facts as Marx deals with in *Capital*. Yet at what a different type of conclusion they arrive! (if one can indeed speak of proposals for social reform as historical "conclusions"). History has since shown who was right, the revolutionary dialectician or the

Fabian evolutionists. But the Fabians did not go wrong through any personal or accidental failings. Indeed we have specially selected names of writers whose ability and conscientious work is not open to question in this way. What hindered them was their inability to understand class struggle, at bottom their failure to look for the "inner contradictory tendencies in the thing." And what enabled Marx to discover "the economic law of motion of modern society" was his possession of a concept "much more comprehensive, much more abundant in content than the current theory of evolution," [9] i.e. the many-sided dialectical theory of development.

V. DIALECTICS AND LOGIC

Dialectics is the Theory of Knowledge (of Hegel and) of Marxism. LENIN.[1]

Dialectics of Thinking

In Chapter III we considered examples of dialectical process in nature, history and human thought, and we examined Lenin's "sixteen points" which are essentially a summary of dialectical method, rules to which thought must conform if it is to reflect the dialectical nature of reality. In this chapter we will deal more explicitly with the thinking activity itself, with the "logic" of the thought process.

The central problem that arises here (in the field of what is called "theory of knowledge" in the philosophy books) is the old question—Are we capable of obtaining a genuine knowledge of reality? And if so, if our thoughts are not mere illusions, if they can reflect a material reality "external" to us (in the sense that its existence is in no way dependent on our sensations) then by what test can the correctness of our thoughts be shown?

To these questions we have already returned the basic materialist answer, and we have seen how at every stage the correctness and adequacy of our conceptions is tested and proved by practice.

But the task of showing in detail how this correspondence between thought and reality is achieved still remains. It raises the vexed question of "truth."

Truth: Absolute and Relative

The mechanist regards human knowledge (ideally, at least) as an exact copy of reality. If he speaks of the "incompleteness" of knowledge the analogy in his mind is a jig-saw puzzle to which some parts are still missing. Thus for example, Bertrand Russell (whose idealist tendencies do not prevent his being a mechanist), looks forward to a time when science will be a completed system of knowledge. In the same way many philosophers in the past put forward their systems as "last words" and "final truths." Even Hegel, who revealed the dialectical development of all preceding philosophy, sought to put forward his own system as the culmination of this development. The common element in all these views is the idea that it is possible to seize hold directly of the "absolute truth," to finalise it in some sort of "system." Error appears to be a mere accident and its complete elimination can be conceived.

On the other hand we have the completely opposite view that "all truth is relative," the view of scepticism, subjectivism, relativism. This view concludes from the practical consideration that science and all human knowledge is continually changing, as well as from typical idealist arguments (like those considered in Chapter I), that there is in fact no such thing as "truth."

Each of these view-points emphasises a fundamental characteristic of human knowledge, but by undialectical concentration on one aspect alone falls into error. Dialectical materialism alone understands how to find the absolute in the relative and the relative in the absolute. Discussing this question (in his *Anti-Dühring*) Engels [2] takes the example of a scientific law, Boyle's law of gas expansion with change of pressure. Experiments made since Boyle's time with more refined apparatus have "refuted" this law, found exceptions to it. But this did not mean that Boyle's law was simply a falsehood—an absolute falsehood because it could not be an absolute truth. Boyle's law was an approximation to the truth, a relative truth that contained, so to speak, a *core of* absolute truth. Its "refutation" meant not the denial of the core of truth contained in it, but its replacement by a *closer* approximation.*

This example of Boyle's law is characteristic of human knowledge in general. In so far as the relative truths with which we are acquainted have an indestructible core to them they give us absolute truth, i.e. reflect objective reality. Our knowledge of absolute truth grows with the accumulation and purification of relative truths. Thus the growth of science does not take place through the haphazard setting-up and knocking-down of theories, a process of destructive, anarchist "negation." Rather is it a process of dialectical growth in which the negation of, say, the Newtonian theory, means the absorption of its content in a higher synthesis, the Einstein theory.

The fundamental criterion which determines this process of growth is of course the *criterion of practice*, the continual comparison of theory with practice which is at the basis of the whole scientific (dialectical materialist) conception of the world.

Discussing this problem of the relation of relative to absolute truth, and arguing especially against the "relativists," Lenin said:

"You will say that this distinction between relative and absolute truth is indefinite. And I shall reply: yes, it is sufficiently 'indefinite' to prevent science from becoming a dogma in the bad sense of the term, from becoming something dead, frozen, ossified; but it is at the same time sufficiently 'definite' to enable us to dissociate ourselves in the most emphatic and irrevocable manner from fideism † and agnosticism, from philosophical ideal-

---

* Boyle's law can be made, in fact, to illustrate the law of the transformation of quantity into quality. According to this law the volume of a gas decreases with the increase of pressure in such a way that it can be calculated theoretically that at a certain pressure a given volume of gas would be reduced to non-existence. This had been advanced as a sceptical argument against Boyle's law. In actual practice, before that hypothetical point can be reached the gas turns into a liquid.

† Fideism, i.e. "Faith-ism."

ism and the sophistry of the followers of Hume and Kant. Here is a boundary which you have not noticed, and not having noticed it, you have fallen into the swamp of reactionary philosophy. It is the boundary between dialectical materialism and relativism." [3]

Dialectics versus Sophistry and Metaphysics

The central problem of truth we have just considered affords an excellent example of the fight which dialectical materialism is continually waging against two opposite kinds of enemies—a "fight on two fronts."

On the one hand we have that metaphysical thinking, referred to in Chapter II, which makes all differences and relations *absolute*, and for this reason is unable to understand the nature of *process*. While it may tolerate such ideas of evolution as amount to simple growth, the appearance of new qualities is inexplicable to it, and development through contradiction pure anathema! On the other hand we have what appears to be the very opposite of metaphysical thinking—the view which holds that "everything is relative." The very philosophy of opportunism! This view pretends to be dialectical, but in fact it loses hold of reality completely and is in a position to justify any conceivable standpoint—and none!

In spite of the polar opposition of these two attitudes, both equally opposed to dialectical materialism, it is quite usual to find them eclectically combined in the same individual (e.g. the case of Bertrand Russell).

The source of all these deviations from dialectics (deviations which lead ultimately to idealism) is explained by Lenin in a splendid passage in his article *On Dialectics:*

"Human knowledge is not (or does not follow) a straight line, but a curve, which endlessly approximates to a series of circles, a spiral. Each fragment, segment, section of this curve can be transformed (transformed one-sidedly) into an independent, complete, straight line, which then (if one does not see the wood for the trees) leads into the quagmire, into clericalism (where it is *reinforced* by the class interests of the ruling classes). Rectilinearity and one-sidedness, stiffness and petrification, subjectivism and subjective blindness—*voilà*—the epistemological roots of idealism. And clericalism (= philosophical idealism), of course, has *epistemological* roots, it is not groundless; it is a *sterile flower* undoubtedly, but it is a sterile flower that grows on the living tree of living, fertile, genuine, powerful, omnipotent, objective, absolute human knowledge." [4]

Dialectical Logic and its Idealist Perversion

To avoid the "stiffness and rigidity" against which Lenin warns us, a special *technique of thinking* is needed, the technique of *dialectical logic* (which approaches questions in the same spirit as we dealt with the relative-absolute nature of truth).

Historically this dialectic dates back to some of the earliest Greek philosophers, but in more recent times it was the German idealist philosophy, above all the work of Hegel, which revived and developed dialectical logic. Hegel's greatest work, his *Science of Logic* (divided into three parts, *The Theory of Being*, *The Theory of Essence*, and *The Theory of the Nation*) contains much of the greatest value even to-day. But the idealist background of this "Logic" makes it impossible to use in its present form, without a radical reconstruction on the materialist basis of the unity of theory and practice.

It was out of the criticism of Hegel's dialectical idealism, as we have already explained, that dialectical materialism arose. Marx and Engels originally formed part of the "left wing" of the Hegelian school, who turned the *dialectic* against their master's *system* and tried to draw revolutionary conclusions instead of the fairly tame political conclusions of their master. But most of these would-be revolutionaries still remained within the idealist orbit, while the quality of their "dialectic" was immeasurably inferior to Hegel.

This fact was ruthlessly exposed in the early polemics of Marx and Engels, particularly in their criticisms of Max Stirner (cf. *The German Ideology*). In view of the fashionable accusation against Marxists to-day, that they prove things "out of their heads", i.e. use their dialectics *idealistically* (cf. Chapter III: *The Law of the Negation of the Negation*, and also Chapter VI) it is useful to recall some of these early Marxist writings.

Max Stirner tried to build the entire history of humanity round the threadbare formula—"(1) realism; (2) idealism; (3) negative unity of both."

> "Thus the whole question in this solemn and tedious historical construction is to find an imposing series of well-sounding names for three categories, which have become so hackneyed that they can no longer appear openly under their own names." [5]

The first form in which these categories appear is as "Child, Youth, Man." Then they are applied more boldly to the divisions of the human race as "Negro, Mongolian, Caucasian" and finally to human history as "Antiquity (the Negroid Caucasians, the Heathen), Modernity (Mongolian Caucasian, the Christian), The Ego ('perfected Christian', 'Caucasian', etc.)." This method has been revived in modern times by the "theoreticians" of Fascism.

This unique method of writing history is varied by other skilful "dialectical" artifices, such as the "synonymics" which are thus described by Marx and Engels:

> "If two words are etymologically connected, or even if they only sound the same, they are made answerable for one another, or if one word has different meanings it will be used accordingly, to read now in the one and now in the other sense, so as

to give the impression that Saint Sancho (Max Stirner) is speaking about one and the same thing in different 'contexts'." [6]

A further trick beloved of idealist philosophers to-day, is juggling with "equations." For instance from the statement "I am not the people" may be deduced the extremely deep philosophical truths "I am the not-people," or "I-not-people," "I am the denial of the people," etc. *ad lib*.

All these and similar artifices, the stock in trade of idealist philosophy (which deduces relations between *things* from relations between their *concepts*) were so well and thoroughly criticised by Marx and Engels over ninety years ago, that nothing remains to the modern "critics" of Marxism than to misapply these arguments to materialistic dialectics. That such criticism cannot be made of the logic of dialectical materialism follows from the very nature of its attempt to *fit thoughts to things*.

While no "systematic" study of dialectical materialist logic exists (just as no book called "Dialectical Materialism" was ever written by Marx, Engels or Lenin) yet this logic is to be studied in *action* in all the works of Marxism, above all in such classics as *Capital*, where it plays an all-important part in the structure of the work.

Dialectics and Formal Logic

The "logic" that we have been discussing is very different from what commonly passes for logic, the *formal logic* which deals with syllogisms and is to be found in the text books. Formal logic is necessary for dealing with the *abstractions* which are formed in the first stage of thinking (Chapter III). The essence of its technique is to keep apart, to prevent confounding the *distinctions* which have been made. It is therefore based on a development of certain very fundamental principles about *identity* and *contradiction*, principles such as the famous "law of the excluded middle" which states that a thing must be one thing (say "A") or not that one thing (say "not A"). It cannot be both "A" and "not A" at the same time.

This logic, which may be termed the "logic of common sense" is perfectly justified and indeed *essential* within certain limits—the same limits as those within which the abstractions it deals with are valid. But just because it is based on taking these abstractions, for the time being, *as absolute*, and because it necessarily overlooks their inter-connections, and the development of one quality or thing into another, formal logic is unable to grasp the inner process of change, to show its dialectical character. For this we require the dialectical logic which has been developed especially in this chapter and in Chapter III. If taken beyond its province formal logic leads to the metaphysical thinking we have criticised.*

The relation of formal logic to dialectics has been well put by Plekhanov: "Just as inertia is a special case of movement so thought in conformity with the rules of formal logic (in conformity with the fundamental laws of thought) is a special case of dialectical thought." [7] Engels has compared the relation to that between lower and higher mathematics. [8]

Dialectical Materialism a Philosophy?

In Chapter II we described dialectical materialism as the "philosophy of the proletariat," and gave reasons for keeping the name "dialectical materialism" and not adopting the loose, ambiguous term "scientific method" which was proposed by Conze. But the question often arises, are we justified in calling dialectical materialism a "philosophy" at all? Do we really need a "philosophy"?

* It is notorious, in practice, how many questions arise which can only be answered correctly by both "*Yes*" and "*No*."

Of course with the old type of "speculative" (idealist) philosophy, which sought to put in the place of scientific truths supposed to be discovered by "Reason," dialectical materialism has nothing in common. It is in this sense the culmination of a chapter in the development of human thought, much as Socialism closes the chapter of social development through class struggle. As Engels puts it:

"... modern materialism is essentially dialectical, and no longer needs any philosophy standing above the other sciences. As soon as each separate science is required to get clarity as to its position in the great totality of things and of our knowledge of things, a special science dealing with this totality is superfluous. What still independently survives of all former philosophy is the science of thought and its laws—formal logic and dialectics. Everything else is merged in the positive science of Nature and History." [9]

If we are ready to call that which deals with "the science of thought and its laws" a *philosophy* (and all previous philosophies have *also* dealt with this, whatever else they may have tried to do) then we must certainly call dialectical materialism a philosophy. There is this further strong reason for the use of the term, that it emphasises the importance of the dialectical outlook and its opposition to metaphysical, idealist philosophies that flourish under capitalism and act as obstacles to the revolutionary movement.

VI. DIALECTICS AND SOPHISTRY*

It is the method of all the sophists of all times to quote examples obviously relating to basically dissimilar cases.[1]   LENIN.

The Idealist Distortion of Dialectics

Dialectics is not magic. It provides no mysterious formulas with occult properties, by means of which most marvellous and unexpected results can be arrived at. The much-misunderstood dialectical laws are—as we explained in Chapter III—merely the most general, universally found characteristics of *process*, and as such they give us a method for investigating processes concretely in various particular fields. But they can in no way eliminate the need for this detailed investigation which falls within the province of one or other of the special sciences. Their value lies in the help that scientific method can give, by pointing to the features of the process under examination which are likely to be important, and in showing the real meaning of the facts discovered.

It is important to emphasise this point because it is common to meet with two opposite kinds of misunderstanding. We have here, in fact, to carry out that "fight on two fronts" explained in Chapter V.

On the one hand we have the *mechanist* view according to which, if dialectics cannot "itself" tell us anything, if detailed scientific investigation is in any case necessary, then we might as well dispense with dialectics as a useless piece of metaphysical luxury and stick to "hard facts." This point of

---

* This chapter appears with apologies to T. A. Jackson who has slaughtered the Philistines on a far grander and more imposing scale in his splendid polemic: *Dialectics—the Logic of Marxism.*

view has already been answered practically, for instance in Chapter IV, where we pointed out how essential is a dialectical grasp of evolution, for a right understanding of social development.

On the other hand we have the view of the *idealist dialecticians* who do in fact try to use dialectics to prove the most extraordinary things by a form of word-play, which can be indulged in with an ease proportioned to one's ignorance of the real subject-matter. We have already come across this "subjective" * form of dialectics in the last chapter, where we saw how mercilessly Marx and Engels, the great *materialist* dialecticians, flayed Max Stirner for attempting to spin the web of history from the single thread, "negation of negation." Such a formula, applied in this way can be used to prove literally *anything*, as Marx and Engels sarcastically pointed out.

In this chapter we are specially concerned with this idealist perversion of dialectics, which is very common among would-be and near-Marxists. Dialectical arguments of this type cease to have any basis, they become mere *sophistry*. We may, in fact, write the equation, *subjective dialectics = sophistry*.

The Misunderstandings of Professor MacMurray

As a first "awful warning" we will consider Professor MacMurray, one of the contributors to that oddly named work, *Aspects of Dialectical Materialism*.† Professor MacMurray's article contains more misunderstandings than can very well be dealt with here, but for us the most important and interesting one is his attempt to press into his service the

---

* "Subjective" because it depends on the arbitrary caprice of the individual thinking subject, not on the real nature of the objects being studied. Materialist dialectics is essentially an "objective."

† Professor MacMurray has also written a *Philosophy of Communism*, developing his views in greater detail.

famous "negation of negation"—and to prove by means of it the inevitability of fascism!

MacMurray performs this feat by pointing out certain alleged *defects* of dialectical materialism, which, he declares—

> "belongs to the biological or organic type of philosophy which is conditioned by the evolutionary problem of the nineteenth century. From this point of view, it falls into the same group as the idealism of Hegel or the realism of Professor Alexander."

Disregarding the fact that Professor MacMurray here "negates" the actual order of historical development (for dialectical materialism and still more Hegelian philosophy, grew up *before* the great discoveries in biology and kindred sciences, which led to the spread of evolutionary views) we come to the *conclusion* he draws from this argument. Since, as MacMurray has told us, dialectical materialism is a biological philosophy, it must ignore the higher "psychological" aspects of man (in other words it is accused of ignoring "individuality," the classic petty-bourgeois objection to Marxism!). But it attempts to make human special activity conscious. It must therefore be "in contradiction with itself." "It is this that gives fascism its chance. It develops the negation within dialectical materialism." The fascist, we are told, "takes his stand on the principles of dialectical materialism." He develops the "biological side" of dialectical materialism, and can only be negated by means of the more adequate philosophy which Professor MacMurray offers to give us. "Our business," he says quite modestly, "is the negation of the negation which will re-establish the fundamental affirmation of dialectical materialism at a higher level."

All this, he hastens to add, does not "justify" fascism. It merely proves (as "the main practical application of this criticism") that it is not *possible* to avoid passing through a fascist stage of development! However, he re-assures us, "we can avoid fascism by passing through the fascist stage under Socialist control" (! !). And in case this should seem a curious assertion, he asks us "to consider what is happening in Russia."

As an example of the wildest sophistry this argument would certainly be hard to beat. Starting out by "negating" the true character of dialectical materialism (which is, as we have seen, by no means a "biological philosophy," but—if one side must be emphasised—is above all rooted in the facts of human society)* he proceeds to prove that history *must* pass through a fascist stage, and then (to safeguard this formula) he is prepared to point either to the workers' dictatorship in the Soviet Union, or presumably to a future Labour government in Britain, as "the fascist stage under Socialist control"! Would one not be correct in calling this philosophy that leads to these remarkable conclusions—"the philosophy of social-fascism"?

How differently dialectical materialism approaches such questions we can see from Dutt's classical study, *Fascism and Social Revolution.* Here we meet, not a few juggling phrases, but a careful and concrete study of fascism "in the totality of its relations." Here the actual class forces are estimated, and it is shown to be possible for the proletariat to avoid passing through the fires of fascism by reforming its class ranks in time on an international scale. But in order to facilitate the development of this class action, one of the first necessities is to clear away the mental cobwebs which keep the proletariat and its allies from a clear understanding of the issues. And such dangerous and muddled notions as we have just examined must be among the first to be swept into the dustbin of history.

---

* Since the Marxian conception of history lays bare the general law of human-social "behaviour" it is more truly "psychological" than most pseudo-psychology.

Lenin "Corrected" or Marxism in the Service of Class Collaboration

The transformation of dialectics into sophistry is not only found in bourgeois professors who are trying to dress up some very old doctrines in dialectical frills. It is also found in some would-be Marxists in the workers' movement who ought to know better. An outstanding example of this type is Fred Casey, whose book, *Method in Thinking*, is announced in the publishers' preface as being "unique as a popular presentation of the much-misunderstood, and as often misrepresented, Dialectical Materialism...." How "unique" we will presently see.

We have already referred to the peculiar confusion which led Casey to advise the proletariat to foster certain brands of idealism. In this passage Casey speaks about "reconciling" idealism and materialism, and he quotes Engels so as to give the entirely false impression that *both* idealism and materialism have been negated, or superseded by dialectical thinking. In the next chapter we will see how this point of view fits in with the general compromising, social-democratic tendencies in philosophy. Here we are more concerned with its origin, which can be traced to certain errors of Josef Dietzgen, whom a certain school of Marxism in Britain has made into *the* authority *par excellence* (rather than Marx and Engels) on dialectics.

These particular errors of Dietzgen are well expressed in the quotation which Casey has chosen for his title-page: "Stable motion and mobile stability; that is the reconciling contradiction, which enables us to reconcile all contradictions."

Thus Dietzgen, and following him Casey, lays the emphasis on the *reconciliation* of the opposites, rather than on their struggle. This point of view leads Casey into a polemic with Lenin, who had stated that, "The unity (coincidence, identity, resultant) of opposites is conditional, temporary, transitory, relative. The struggle of mutually exclusive opposites is absolute, just as development and motion are absolute." [2]

Casey cannot stomach the "one-sidedness" of this view. He maintains that the "unity" of the opposites is as absolute as their struggle, and accuses Lenin of being "not very clear in dialectical theory," in fact of being "a bad dialectician." This error, we are told, "led him astray on the question of mind and matter, notwithstanding that in matters of revolutionary political expediency he was a model worth studying." In the next chapter we will find *who* was "led astray on the question of mind and matter." Here we are merely concerned to vindicate Lenin on this particular point, and to suggest that possibly his correct political practice ("revolutionary political expediency"—translated into the language of the opportunists!) may have had some relation to a correct political theory.

Curious that a dialectician of Comrade Casey's calibre, with his modest efforts at correcting Lenin, not to speak of Marx and Engels, should have overlooked the dialectical inter-relation of theory and practice!

We can best clear up the point at issue by taking an example, say the example of "grim and deadly capitalism" given by Casey himself. To say that considered as a static "thing," it is "relative," means that it can be regarded as a fixed system of society (*apart from the developing class struggle within it*), only from a very limited, restricted standpoint, that of one who thinks entirely within the capitalist epoch, and even within the capitalism of a particular period. But if capitalism is considered from the point of view of the developing universe as a whole, of its relation to past and to future societies, i.e. from the most "absolute" standpoint that we can rise to, then it is the *struggle* of opposites that becomes fundamental. This should make clear why we say—and what we mean when we say—that the unity of opposites is "conditional, temporary, transitory, relative," while their struggle is "absolute, just as development and motion are absolute."

Without understanding this point it is impossible to understand the dialectics of absolute and relative, or why we may say "the absolute is contained in the relative" but not say simply "the absolute is the relative." Failure to grasp this leads to a loss of dialectical balance, to dialectics being transformed into a kind of verbal-acrobatics round such themes as "the absolute is the relative and the relative is the absolute," to which Casey treats us in such great profusion in his book. In this he is again following the mistakes of Josef Dietzgen, whom Marx criticised for his "lack of dialectical development and his way of going round in a circle." [3]

The Marxism of Decayed German Social Democracy

The most commonly met forms of sophistry have a simpler origin—are less "sophisticated"—than the arguments we have been considering. "It is the method of all the sophists of all times to quote examples obviously relating to basically dissimilar cases." An example of this kind of sophistry at its crudest is the trick which Conze (Ex-German Social Democrat now turned pedlar of anti-communist "Marxism" in the British Labour Movement) plays with the expression "state capitalism" in his recently published *Introduction to Dialectical Materialism*. Conze reproduces Lenin's classification of the *five economic forms* to be found in the N.E.P. Russia of 1921, which included such differing systems as self-sufficing peasant production, simple peasant production for the market, private capitalism, *state capitalism* ("capitalism under the control and regulation of the proletarian state" [4]) as Lenin phrased it, a system of economic relations dominated by "concessions," i.e.

industry leased out to private capitalists and Socialists. Since then, as Stalin was able to report at the Seventeenth Congress of the C.P.S.U., "capitalist economy in the U.S.S.R. has already been liquidated and the individual peasant sector in the rural districts has been forced back to a secondary position . . . while the fifth social-economic system—the Socialist system, now has unchallenged predominance, and is the sole commanding force in the whole of the national economy." [5]

Conze is willing to agree that there has been a big transformation in the U.S.S.R.—but he thinks it should be described somewhat "differently" from Stalin. "In the meantime," he says, "private capitalism has been destroyed almost completely, but bureaucratic state capitalism has grown immensely. It is very unscientific to talk about the gigantic steps towards Socialism in the U.S.S.R. and to forget the other factors in the situation, especially factor 4 (i.e. state capitalism)."

This argument is almost the most perfect example of sophistry, for it entirely depends on the confusion about the meaning of "state capitalism" natural to a bourgeois theorist but unforgivable in a "Marxist." When the capitalist state takes over an industry we know that this is not yet Socialism; it may justly be called *state capitalism*. In a Social state, however, industry run by the state is *Socialist industry* in the only possible meaning of the term. The term "state capitalism" applies (in the sense above-explained, which was coined by Lenin) only to that state-controlled capitalism which was tolerated in Russia at the beginning of N.E.P. but has since been liquidated. At least we are forced to this conclusion if we use the terms in the sense that Lenin used them. There remains the possibility that Conze is using them in a different sense— the sense in which the fascists speak of the Soviet system as "bureaucratic state capitalism"—but in this case it is clear that his argument is not only an unspeakable distortion but serves the very worst reactionary ends. Conze implies the query, "What worker of sense will make sacrifices to defend a system dominated by this bureaucratic state capitalism?" His malevolent hatred of the U.S.S.R. comes out in all he writes.

In another section of this book Conze treats the "unity of opposites" in much the same spirit as Casey, and manages by means of it to find a "class harmony" which explains fascism. It is quite evident that this "treatment" of dialectics converts it into the most devitalising form of mental poison. Its presence in the writings of Conze, who as an old German social-democrat is far from being a political innocent, is to say the least, somewhat sinister.

Dialectics and the International Situation

The statement of Lenin's which we took as the motto of this chapter was originally directed against the opportunists of the Second International who justified their participation in the Imperialist War by appealing to the attitude of Marx and Engels in a situation before the development of imperialism. "Marx and Engels," they declared, "were ready to take part in a capitalist war, to decide which belligerent represented the forces of progress on balance, and therefore we should do the same." They totally ignored the *new features* of the situation, which made it meaningless to decide which group of aggressor powers represented "progress," and made "transform the Imperialist war into civil war," the plain and immediate slogan for the Socialists of all countries.

To-day the very *same mistake*, in essence, but from the opposite angle is made by those sections of the Socialist movement who have awakened (rather late, in some cases) to the facts of imperialism, but have totally failed to see such new factors in the world situation as the Soviet Union and fascism, and still try to repeat blindly the slogans of twenty years ago.

Some of these newly-born "Marxists" (who are really in complete innocence of Marxism-Leninism) would be very shocked to read, say, the advice given by Engels [6] to the German social-democrats in 1870—qualified support of the war to repel the aggressor *plus* maintaining the independence of the working class—and would no doubt be very scornful of this last bit ("for how can the working class have an independent line unless it opposes the Government on *every* issue?").

Of course no real Marxist would seek to justify the tactics to be applied in the international situation to-day by appealing to the slogans of 1870, any more than to the slogans of 1914. What matters is that we should carry out the fundamental rule of Marxism and examine each and every question *concretely*. Long ago Engels complained that the opportunists "give prominence to generalised and abstract political questions, thereby concealing the immediate concrete problems, which automatically arise at the first outbreak of events, and at the first political crisis." [7]

If we look at the situation in this concrete way we will reach conclusions very different from the abstract generalities of the I.L.P. In the words of Dimitroff:

"It is true that imperialist wars are the product of capitalism, that only the overthrow of capitalism will put an end to all war; but it is likewise true that the masses of working people can obstruct imperialist war by their militant action.

"To-day the world is not what it was in 1914.

"To-day on one-sixth part of the globe there exists a powerful proletarian state that relies on the material strength of victorious socialism. Guided by Stalin's wise peace policy, the Soviet Union has already more than once brought to nought the aggressive plans of the instigators of war.

"To-day the world proletariat, in its struggle against war, has at its disposal not only its weapon of mass action, as it did in 1914. To-day the mass struggle of the international working class against war is coupled with the influence of the Soviet Union as a State, of its powerful Red Army, the most important guardian of the peace.

"To-day the working class is not under the exclusive influence of Social-Democracy participating in a bloc with the bourgeoisie, as was the case in 1914. To-day there is the World Communist Party, the Communist International. To-day the bulk of the Social-Democratic workers are turning to the Soviet Union, to its policy of peace, to a united front with the Communists. To-day the peoples of the colonial and semi-colonial countries do not regard their liberation as a hopeless cause." [8]

It is in this concrete way that dialectical materialists, from Marx and Engels to Lenin and Stalin and Dimitroff, have always solved problems. To those theorising fanatics who hang on to their sacred formulas (which are supposed to contain the "absolute truth," valid under all conditions) we would reply in the words of Engels:

"What all these Gentlemen lack is dialectics."

VII. THE PHILOSOPHICAL
STRUGGLE TO-DAY

*Recent philosophy is as partisan as it was two thousand years
ago.* LENIN.

Ideology and the Class Struggle under Imperialism

Each special phase in the development of capitalism and the
working-class struggle gives rise to its own particular forms
of social consciousness, to its own "ideology." This is but an
illustration of the social dialectics studied in Chapter IV. It
was true in the early days of capitalism, when the progressive
role of the bourgeoisie was mirrored in the materialistic tendency of its philosophy. It remains true to-day in the epoch
of imperialism, which is parasitic monopoly-capitalism in de-
cay, imperialism which is (in Lenin's words) "the eve of proletarian revolution."

We may distinguish three main characteristics of the present epoch, each of which is clearly expressed in present-day
social consciousness.

There is in the first place the parasitic, decadent character
of imperialism, which grows in the same proportion as class
and national oppression increases. This leads to the passing
over of a considerable section of the bourgeoisie to reactionary,
mystical-religious tendencies, the very tendencies against which
the older thinkers of the bourgeoisie had fought. At the same
time we get the emergence of a new materialism, the revolutionary dialectical materialism that inspires the workers'
struggle.

Secondly, we have the important fact that the conditions
of the imperialist epoch lead to a split in the working-class

85

movement, a split between the opportunist "aristocracy of labour" (and those influenced by it) and the revolutionary section of the workers. The opportunists adapt themselves to capitalism and sacrifice the general interests of the working class so long as their own special interests are maintained. In this way they form an indispensable buttress of capitalism. Since their whole practice is based on a desire to compromise, it is not surprising that *compromising philosophies* should flourish under their encouragement.

Thirdly, as a result of this split and the consequent disorganisation of the workers as a class, it becomes possible (if the workers do not reform their ranks in time) for the bourgeoisie to pass over to the open, fascist dictatorship—whose "ideology" is expressed in the burning of books, in hysterical screaming about "blood and land," in the degenerate, antiscientific mysticism of the fascist "racial" theories.

In this chapter we will consider the way in which these factors get expressed in the contemporary struggle of philosophical tendencies.

The Philosophy of Compromise

Towards the end of the nineteenth and the beginning of the twentieth centuries (about the time that capitalism developed its imperialist phase) there spread over Europe and America a philosophical tendency based on the attempt to overcome the old opposition between materialism and idealism. This "Machist" tendency (so-called after its most systematic German representative Ernst Mach) was especially welcomed by the opportunists in the Socialist movement and spread to Russia, where it called forth the most devastating criticism from Lenin. We will examine it mainly in the work of the most prominent British representative of this school, Bertrand Russell. The student who reads Lenin's *Materialism and Empirio-*

Criticism will find that Lenin's arguments against Mach apply to Russell almost word for word.

Bertrand Russell has in several places given a good account of his philosophical relationships. Thus in an essay on *Philosophy in the Twentieth Century* (included in his *Sceptical Essays*) he says:

> "Meanwhile from many directions a philosophy grew up which is often described as realism. . . . It is not necessarily realistic since it is in some forms compatible with Berkelian idealism [only in some forms?—D. G.]. . . . It tends more and more to the adoption of James' view that the fundamental stuff of the world is neither mental nor material, but something simpler and more fundamental, out of which both mind and matter are constructed."

Elsewhere, Russell calls this view "Neutral Monism," and states that it "is suggested in Mach's *Analysis of Sensations*, developed in William James' *Essays in Radical Empiricism*, and advocated by John Dewey, as well as by Professor R. B. Perry and other American realists" (*Outlines of Philosophy*).

It is interesting to examine these philosophical associates of Russell, the would-be rationalist, hostile to "intoxicated speculation." In the first place we have Russell's admission that the movement of which he forms part is related to Berkeley (the philosophising bishop we remember from Chapter I). And it is certainly true that the Machians derive from Berkeley and Hume their arguments against the "dogmatism" of matter, quite in the spirit explained above in Chapter I.

But secondly we have the significant fact that William James, whom Russell calls the founder of both "realism" and "pragmatism," openly set out to find a philosophical justification for theology. The curious thing is that Russell exposes the trick by which James attempted to do this—"He advocated pragmatism as a means of presenting religious hopes as scientific hypotheses" (*Sceptical Essays*). But to Russell this tendency in James appears a mere accident. He does not see that the theological leanings of his associates are the natural accompaniment of a fundamentally idealist tendency in philosophy. He does not see that he has merely taken the first steps on the slippery slope down towards idealism, and that some of his associates have slid further down this path.*

The parallel between Russell and Mach is often astonishingly close. Mach wrote: "Not the things (bodies) but colours, sounds, pressures, spaces, times (what we usually call sensations) are the actual elements of the world." (*Die Mechanik in ihrer Entwicklung.*) And Russell says: " . . . the actual data in sensation, the immediate objects of sight or touch or hearing, are extra-mental, purely physical, and among the ultimate constituents of matter." (*Mysticism and Logic.*) If at first sight Russell's statement might seem "materialistic," further reading shatters this illusion. Russell is good enough to agree with common sense that what is seen is physical, only—"it is probably wrong in supposing that it continues to exist when we are no longer looking at it." (!)

Thus Mach and Russell have both the same starting point, they take sensations or sense-data, that is to say, "subjective," mental phenomena, as the *ultimate elements in the universe*. This starting point is pure *subjective idealism* (see Chapter I), and their whole philosophy from this point onwards may be defined as an elaborate attempt, by means of the most tortuous, involved kind of confusion, to avoid the clearly solipsist conclusions implied in their starting point.

In their later works both writers learn to conceal this starting point more carefully. Mach talks vaguely about "world

* A. N. Whitehead, who formerly collaborated with Russell and is now a complete mystic, is another glaring example.

elements," and Russell speaks of "sensibilia" or of "particulars" (he is constantly changing the name) which are supposed to constitute that "more fundamental stuff" out of which both "mind" and "matter" are constructed. But whenever the precise nature of these "elements" and "particulars" is examined more closely they are found to reduce either directly to elements of sensation, or to elements only "definable" in terms of sensation, thus clearly revealing the subjective idealist roots of this "neutral" philosophy.

"A red thread that runs through *all* the writings of *all* the Machians is the stupid claim to have 'risen above' materialism and idealism, to have transcended this 'obsolete' antithesis; but *in fact* the whole fraternity are *continually* sliding into idealism and are conducting a steady and incessant struggle against materialism." [1] This sentence of Lenin's, written some twenty years before the most typical of Russell's "neutral monist" writings, sounds almost uncanny to-day. It is a measure both of the "up-to-dateness" of the Leninist critique of imperialism, and of the essential inability of the bourgeoisie to produce anything new in this, the final stage of capitalism.

In the case of Russell it is possible to see very clearly the connection between his general philosophy and his political outlook, which he has defined in these terms—"I am a British whig, with a British love of compromise" (*Sceptical Essays*). Subjectively, Russell does not *want* to support capitalism, any more than he wants to be an idealist (where he *desires* to stand philosophically he has expressed by saying, "I am not a materialist, but I am still further from idealism"). But, objectively, when Russell misunderstands and misrepresents Marxism in so many of his writings, and when he looks to President Roosevelt rather than to the Soviet Union to show humanity the way forward, there is no doubt that he does render such support. But against this must be set the fact, of growing importance to-day, of Russell's genuine hatred of the crude fascist forms of capitalist rule, as also his stand (presently to be shown) against the most aggressive forms of philosophical reaction.

Certainly Russell cannot be accused of *consistency*, either in his philosophy or in his politics. Philosophically he is more naïve in his earlier writings, and takes scarcely any trouble to conceal their solipsist implications. His later writings (*The Analysis of Matter*) incline more to a kind of *"Mechanical Agnosticism,"* if one can use the term. All of Russell's work is dominated by that "metaphysical" thinking which has so long survived in England (never having succumbed to the German idealist philosophy). About Russell one is impelled to repeat what Marx said so long ago of Proudhon: "He wants to be the synthesis— he is a composite error. He wants to soar as a scientist above the bourgeois and the proletarians; he is merely the petty bourgeois, continually tossed back and forth between capital and labour, political economy and communism." [2]

Social-Democracy and Philosophy

It is not surprising that the opportunist, "Machist" philosophy should be so popular among the modern apostles of class compromise—the Social-Democrats. Examples from all countries could be given to illustrate this widespread connection of Machism and Reformism. In this section we will deal with an attempt to smuggle this philosophy into the British workers' movement disguised as Marxism.

The author of this remarkable attempt is no other than the same Casey whose views on the absolute character of the unity of opposites we were compelled to criticise in the last chapter. As we pointed out there, Casey understands this unity to be a principle by which any pair of opposites can be "reconciled" in something higher—a purely *eclectic* conception which has nothing in common with dialectics.*

This view leads Casey, exactly in the spirit of Russell and Mach, to rebuke both materialists and idealists for being "one-enders" and to put forward his brand of "dialectics" or "proletarian Monism," exactly as they put forward an admittedly "non-proletarian allegedly *neutral* Monism," as a philosophy that is superior to both materialism and idealism. "Of course, if we still like to use the words 'materialism' and 'idealism' by way of accommodation to the needs of those who as yet do not understand dialectics [e.g. Marx, Engels, Lenin, etc., who continually described their method as *materialist*!! D. G.] all well and good" (*Method in Thinking*, p. 152).

Casey's method (guaranteed not "one-ended") leads him to such gems of lucidity as the following: " . . . there is no 'pure' thought, which means thought without any object to be thought about. *Nor is there any object without thought.* Even an 'unknown' object is known to be unknown, and is also known to be an object. Therefore every object is really a two-fold affair. It is a subjective-objective thing or an objective-subjective thing, just whichever way one likes to put it (ibid., p. 15)." This may be the purest "Monism," it is certainly *idealism*, but whether it is "proletarian" in any other sense than "destitute" beyond redemption by the P.A.C. may be doubted.

The same method makes him especially scornful of "the big boys who are profoundly educated" who say that, "Matter is a condition for the existence of mind, but mind is not a condition for the existence of matter" (ibid., p. 57). From his superior Monist position Casey tells us that "matter" and "existence" have both the same meaning, and that "mind" is just a

---

* This view is in fact the *precise opposite* of the dialectical view, according to which it is the *struggle* of the opposites which leads to the *breaking* of their unity and the emergence of the "new." Nor can these opposite views—the *dialectic* of Marx and the *eclectic* of Casey—be "reconciled."

part of "matter" (whatever that may mean) (ibid., p. 51). Elsewhere he says that "heat" and "motion" are *parts* of matter—a form of confusion into which even the worse vulgarisers of the old mechanical materialism seldom descended.

There is no doubt that Casey has been led into these confusions by certain mistakes of the afore-mentioned Josef Dietzgen, who also tried to give the concept of matter a more comprehensive meaning so that to it would belong "all the phenomena of reality, also our force of thinking." Lenin criticised this view of Dietzgen as it abolished the basis of the distinction between mind and matter, and obscured the way in which the phenomena of sensation and consciousness arise as functions of matter at a certain stage in its development.

But in the case of Dietzgen these were mainly terminological errors, as Lenin recognised. It was only later that they were seized on by certain "Marxists" eager to abandon Marxism for Machism, and made into a principle (called "proletarian monism" by Josef Dietzgen's son—Eugene Dietzgen—who offered this electic philosophy as a means of reconciling the reformist and revolutionary wings of Social-Democracy).

Elsewhere Dietzgen fully recognised the importance of "the basic question of philosophy." "Indeed," he said, "the question as to which is primary, mind or matter, contains also the problem as to the right way to justice and truth." Alas that Casey through being "led astray on the question of mind and matter" should also lose the "right way to justice and truth!" and land himself in the company of all the bourgeois moralists from Bentham to Hitler! But such is the case, for rejecting the Marxist, materialist way of putting the question in terms of class interests, Casey adopts the hypocritical bourgeois definition of morality (due especially to Bentham) "that which is moral, is, as said, that which serves the general interests" (ibid., p. 164). That this vague phrase, "the general interests," conceals the absolute opposition of the interests of two mutually opposed classes in present-day society, for which reason it is always used by bourgeois theorists and figures in the Nazi Programme, and also that Marxist criticism has always been directed against this "above the parties" attitude, these things appear quite unknown to Casey, so far has he sunk into the swamp of commonplace bourgeois Philistinism.

"Another warning. . . . The road away from Marx to 'Dietzgenism' and 'Machism' is a road into the morass, not for individuals, not for Tom, Dick and Harry, but for the movement" (Lenin).[3] Casey, and those following him, have certainly taken this "road into the morass."

VIII. PROBLEMS OF SOCIALIST CULTURE

The Unity of Theory and Practice in Socialist Culture

Up to now most of our political illustrations of dialectical materialism have been drawn from the problems of working-class struggle under capitalism. In this chapter we will deal (though very briefly) with some of the problems that arise on the cultural field after the workers have conquered power, and we will see how the same revolutionary philosophy lights the way to their solution.

We have already referred to the fatal disease of capitalist culture—*the divorce of theory from practice*—which arises from the special form of the division of labour under capitalism. A further result of the capitalist division of labour is the universal "compartmentalising" of activities, which gets expressed on both practical and theoretical fields. This fact is recognised by many scientific workers to-day. It has been stressed by Professor Levy in a recent book:

> "Within a movement such as Science, separated into its almost water-tight compartments of Mathematics, Physics, Chemistry, Biology, Psychology, Engineering, etc., the values that are attached to individual developments bear little relation to the wider movement. Each group pursues its way along its own tangent, setting up its own criteria of importance. In an environment where the danger is ever present that only those fields of study may be permitted or encouraged that bear an immediate relation to the industrial practice of the day, this acts as a distinct safeguard, but it inevitably builds up systems of values in each subject that cannot be reconciled as between subjects. That reconciliation will be effected only when scientists recognise the social roots and the social function of their movement. There is no organised body that represents them in this respect." [1]

This compartmentalising of activities forms a natural basis for the narrow, "metaphysical" or *mechanist* outlook, which we found to be so persistent a feature of bourgeois thought. But just as dialectical materialism overcomes this metaphysical isolation in thought and sees the parts of the world in their real inseparability, so does Socialist culture based on planned production (both practical and theoretical) overcome the narrowness of the bourgeois division of labour, abolishing its rigid compartments and above all its separation of theory from practice. All these features of Socialist culture may be seen to-day in the Soviet Union, and indeed exemplified in the most varied ways. We will consider only a few examples, chosen almost at random.

Here is a Soviet Academician, speaking at a conference of the foremost live-stock breeders with Party and Government leaders (from the *Moscow Daily News*, February 21st, 1936):

> "I believe that the duty of scientific workers at present consists in immediately studying and generalising the vast amount of experience accumulated by the practical work of Stakhanovites. The methods of studying this experience are suggested by life itself. While up to this time scientific workers and practical workers who work in livestock breeding stalls have worked separately, I am now calling on both scientific workers and practical workers to co-operate, and in my old age, I myself will give a personal example of how this work can be done. I, for instance, am working with Comrade Nadezhda Petrovna Persihantseva (a milkmaid) on a book—"How to obtain the highest milk yield from a cow." And I believe that should we succeed in this joint work —and I have no doubt we shall—we will have such a work as I have not yet created in all the thirty-six years of my scientific and practical activity."

But scientific theory and practice have not only to be brought closer together in this way. Science itself has to be brought closer to the masses by being linked up with art and literature.

Here also great developments are taking place in the Soviet Union, some of which are referred to in an interesting article in the collection *Literature of the Peoples of the U.S.S.R.*[2]

"Socialist Realism" in Literature

The same unity of theory and practice which drives forward the development of Soviet science inspires in different ways the growth of Soviet literature. This was one of the main themes of the recent (1934) All-Union Soviet Writers' Congress (cf. especially the contributions of Gorky).

The history of the literature of class society shows how it has become separated from the life of the masses. Conversely, the history of Soviet literature, short though its period of existence has been, is the history of the increasing approach of literature to the masses, of its attempt to portray consciously the struggles of a people building Socialist society.

Soviet literature has grown, as the young revolutionary literature in the capitalist countries is still growing, from the merging of two streams which mutually fertilise each other—from revolutionary writers coming over from the bourgeoisie to the side of the workers on the one hand, and from proletarian writers directly springing from the ranks of the working class and seeking to express its aspirations on the other.

Soviet literature is developing under the slogan of "Socialist Realism," which is simply the dialectical materialist world outlook, developed and applied in literature. As the name suggests, there have been other brands of "realism," just as there have been other kinds of materialism besides dialectical materialism. But, fundamentally, these other brands of literary realism reduce everything to the standard of bourgeois "individualism"—"the outlook of the single individual in 'civil society'," which as Marx explained in his *Theses on Feuerbach*, was the standpoint of the old materialism. The new materialism transcends this individualist standpoint. Its outlook is that of the new materialism—the outlook of "human society or socialised humanity."

Bourgeois realism, which has been connected historically with the progressive aspects of bourgeois society, is now giving way everywhere to "escapism," to the flight from reality. Literature which still desires to be realist can remain so only by reflecting in some way the profound social contradictions of to-day. And an adequate picture of these contradictions must show them not only "in themselves," but also as expressed in the trends of development arising out of them. That is to say, such realism must be essentially dialectical, at bottom it must approach the method of Socialist realism.

Socialist realism means not only the grasping of reality as it is, but the understanding of whither it is moving and why. It is moving towards Socialism, it is moving towards the victory of the international proletariat. And a work of art created by a Socialist realist is one which shows to what that conflict of contradictions is leading which the artist has seen in life and reflects in his work.

Towards Communist Society

By following this road of breaking down the barriers between scientific theory and practice, and between the different sciences themselves, dialectical materialism has the tremendous task of showing the way to a *complete reconstruction of science*. Such a reconstructed science will not only for the first time present a unified picture of the world, instead of the series of mutually conflicting pictures that we get at present (as Levy pointed out). It will also, at least in its basic elements, become the common property of the whole of mankind, the first common human outlook in history.

In this way will be realised those features of the higher phase of *Communist society* which were foreseen by Marx:

"In a higher phase of communist society, after the enslaving subordination of individuals under division of labour, and therewith also the antithesis between mental and physical labour, has vanished; after labour, from a mere means of life, has itself become the prime necessity of life; after the productive forces have also increased with the all-round development of the individual, and all the springs of co-operative wealth flow more abundantly—only then can the narrow horizon of bourgeois right be fully left behind and society inscribe on its banners: from each according to his ability, to each according to his needs!" [3]

The development of Stakhanovism in the Soviet Union, by producing the abundance of goods which is the necessary material basis of Communism, and by simultaneously breaking down the barriers between theory and practice, is pioneering the way to this higher state of society when "the narrow horizon of bourgeois right can be fully left behind."

Socialism and Morality

As the Socialist attitude to questions of ethics and morality is often misunderstood it is important to deal specially with this subject. "It is frequently the bourgeoisie which makes the charge that we Communists deny all morality. That is one of their methods of confusing the issue, of throwing dust into the eyes of the workers and peasants. In what sense do we deny ethics, morals? In the sense in which they are preached by the bourgeoisie, a sense which deduces these morals from God's commandments." [4]

Marxism sees that moral codes like other branches of ideology are rooted in the interests of some particular class. In thus exposing the origin of *bourgeois* morality it naturally helps the proletariat to fight against its enslaving influence. But this attitude has nothing in common with the petty-bourgeois, nihilist opposition to *all* morality, any more than the Marxist opposition to the bourgeois State is to be confused with the petty-bourgeois, anarchist opposition to the State in the abstract. As on all other issues so here in the field of morality Marxism has to carry on a "fight on two fronts."

The Socialist movement, itself, which is based on the class struggle, needs an ethical and moral outlook (or "code") dictated by the interests of that class struggle. The development of a strong sense of class solidarity, and the willingness of the individual to subordinate his private, temporary interests to the lasting interests of the class struggle (which are also the *permanent* interests of the individual) is indeed very important. It is specially important in the case of the revolutionary party, which has at all stages of the fight to represent the class interests of the workers, and through them the future of mankind. Clearly the revolutionary party can tolerate no petty-bourgeois individualism in its midst which will weaken its fighting capacity.

This *Socialist morality* which first springs from the class struggle under capitalism, only attains full flower in Socialist society. But it does not become static even then. With each phase of Socialist development there is a corresponding development in moral conceptions, in Socialist "public opinion." This is illustrated by the change in the attitude to labour in the Soviet Union in recent years. It is also illustrated by recent changes in the Soviet Marriage Code, which have come as a result of growing Socialist prosperity and the increasing value of human beings. It is typical of the restrictedness of even "advanced" bourgeois thought to-day that the liberal newspapers commenting on this change could find no reason—in a land of boundless opportunities for all, of all-round shortage of people —to desire more people except for use as cannon-fodder!

BIBLIOGRAPHICAL APPENDIX

In the previous chapters we have made many references to the classical works of Marxism-Leninism. For the convenience of students these references are collected together here under chapter-heads, and in the case of each chapter a brief summary is given of the most useful (and available) books dealing with its subject-matter.

For a general introduction to dialectical materialism, it is impossible to recommend anything better than those three chapters which Frederick Engels took from his book *Anti-Dühring* and published separately under the title *Socialism: Utopian and Scientific*. The complete *Anti-Dühring* is a more many-sided exposition of the Marxist world outlook than this extract, but because of the greater breadth of subjects dealt with it is also more difficult.

Almost as clear and simple as *Socialism: Utopian and Scientific* is that other book of Engels, *Ludwig Feuerbach and the Outcome of Classical German Philosophy*, which shows how Marx and Engels themselves reached the standpoint of Dialectical Materialism. Only it must be read (and this warning applies to other books mentioned in the Appendix) in the *correct* translation (published by International Publishers), not in the distorted form that helped for many years to spread theoretical confusion in the English-speaking world.

The inseparable unity of all the "aspects" of Marxism, and the position of dialectics as "the theory of knowledge of Marxism," is dealt with very concisely in Lenin's Encyclopedia article entitled *The Teachings of Karl Marx* (International Publishers) also reproduced in the collection of Lenin articles published as *Marx-Engels-Marxism* (International Publishers). The most important section of this article is contained—along with extracts from many other writings mentioned in this appendix—in the *Handbook of Marxism* edited by Emile Burns (International Publishers).

For those whose approach to Marxism has already been confused by the various self-styled "explanations" of Marxist philosophy current to-day, we recommend T. A. Jackson's brilliant (and witty) polemic, *Dialectics: The Logic of Marxism* (International Publishers). This should help to dispel the fog. It is one of the few popularisations of Marxism in English which is of real use to the student. A general introduction to philosophy from the Marxist standpoint is *What is Philosophy?* by Howard Selsam (International Publishers).

INTRODUCTION

The relation of theory to practice is so central a question of Marxism that it is difficult to give special references. Under one head or another it is dealt with throughout this book.

We may, however, specially mention Marx's *Theses on Feuerbach* (Appendix to Engels' *Ludwig Feuerbach*, etc.) and the exposition which T. A. Jackson gives of them in *Dialectics: The Logic of Marxism*.

(1)   Hessen. Essay on Newton in *Science at the Crossroads* (Kniga).

(2)   Engels. *Peasant War in Germany* (International Publishers). Quoted in Lenin's *What is to be Done?*, p. 29 (International Publishers).

CHAPTER ONE

The issue of Materialism versus Idealism is dealt with most fundamentally in Engels' *Ludwig Feuerbach and the Outcome of Classical German Philosophy* (especially in the *second* section). The basic materialist standpoint of Marx and Engels appears clearly in all their writings and is often specially elucidated, as in *The German Ideology* (International Publishers), and Marx's preface to the second edition of *Capital*. How the materialism of a modern natural scientist approaches dialectical materialism when he is not afraid of the social conclusions to be drawn from it, may be seen in the recent writings of Professor H. Levy, especially *The Universe of Science* (Watts), *Science in an Irrational Society* (Watts), and *Thinking* (Newnes), also in Professor J. B. S. Haldane's book *The Marxist Philosophy and the Sciences* (Random House), and Marcel Prenant's *Biology and Marxism* (International Publishers). The agnostic, sceptical philosophy described in this chapter has been splendidly refuted by Engels, cf. his introduction to *Socialism: Utopian and Scientific* (International Publishers).

(1) Engels. *Ludwig Feuerbach*, etc., p. 30.
(2) Engels. *Ludwig Feuerbach*, etc., p. 31.
(3) Marx-Engels. *The German Ideology*, p. 6.
(4) Levy. *The Universe of Science*, p. 20.
(5) Lenin. *Karl Marx* (*Marx-Engels-Marxism*, p. 11).

CHAPTER TWO

How dialectical materialism arose from the "negation" of Hegelian philosophy is the main theme of Engels' *Ludwig Feuerbach*, etc., and the appendices given with the new International Publishers' edition amplify this history.

The relation of dialectical materialism to the older French materialism is more particularly dealt with by Plekhanov in his *Essays in the History of Materialism* (John Lane).

The dialectical criticism of mechanist thinking is to be found throughout the writings of Marx and Engels, e.g. in the *Selected Correspondence of Marx and Engels* (International Publishers), and in Engels' *Anti-Dühring* (International Publishers).

(1) Marx. Preface to 2nd edition of *Capital, Vol. I* (International Publishers, 1939 edition, p. xxx).
(2) Marx. Quoted by Engels in his introduction to *Socialism: Utopian and Scientific*, p. x. Also, see Engels, *Ludwig Feuerbach*, etc. (Appendix C, p. 84).
(3) Holbach. Quoted by Plekhanov. *Essays in the History of Materialism*, p. 13.
(4) Ibid., p. 167.
(5) Ibid., p. 167.
(6) Engels. *Ludwig Feuerbach*, etc., p. 53.
(7) Ibid., p. 53.
(8) Ibid., p. 54.
(9) Ibid., p. 54.
(10) Engels. *Anti-Dühring* (1939 edition), p. 152.

CHAPTER THREE

To study more adequately the "general nature of dialectics," and follow up many questions just touched on in this chapter, the reader is advised to turn at once to Engels' *Anti-Dühring*, particularly to Part I: *Philosophy*. Chapter V of T. A. Jackson's *Dialectics* (on the Dialectics of Nature and History) contains much useful material, especially in connection with recent scientific developments. Plekhanov's essay, *Sudden Changes in Nature and History*, published in *Fundamental Problems of Marxism* (International Publishers), brings out very clearly some essential features of dialectics.

(1) Engels. *Natur Dialektik*. Marx-Engels Archiv II. Band. An English translation of this will shortly be published by International Publishers.

(2) Engels. Appendix B to *Ludwig Feuerbach*, etc.

(3) Engels. *Anti-Dühring*, p. 16.

(4) Engels. *Natur Dialektik*.

(5) Hegel. *The Logic of Hegel*, translated by Wallace, p. 222. (Clarendon Press.)

(6) Bernal. *Aspects of Dialectical Materialism*, p. 99. (Watts.)

(7) Lenin. *Philosophic Notebooks*, quoted by V. Adoratsky with other similar remarks in *Dialectical Materialism*, p. 28. (International Publishers.)

(8) Lenin. *On Dialectics*. (*Selected Works*, Vol. XI, p. 81.)

(9) Kuno Fischer. Quoted by Plekhanov, *Fundamental Problems of Marxism*, p. 123.

(10) Marx. *Capital, Vol. I* (International Publishers, p. 789).

(11) Engels. *Anti-Dühring*, p. 147.

(12) Lenin. *Philosophic Notebooks*. (German edition only.) The translation given here is slightly modified from that which originally appeared in the *Labour Monthly* (March 1932) and is reproduced in *Aspects of Dialectical Materialism*, p. 14.

(13) Levy. Article in *Aspects of Dialectical Materialism*, p. 18.

CHAPTER FOUR

Social dialectics—more particularly the dialectics of capitalist society—are naturally the theme of most Marxist writings. At the bottom of the concrete study of social dialectics contained in the historical studies of Marxism lies "the economic law of motion of modern (i.e. bourgeois) society," which was most thoroughly investigated by Marx in *Capital*. The student who has time should make an attempt to read at least the *historical* sections of the first volume of *Capital*—(cf. Marx's advice in *Letters to Kugelmann*, p. 54 (International Publishers).

(1) Marx. *Theses on Feuerbach*, Appendix A to Engels' *Ludwig Feuerbach*, etc., p. 75.

(2) Engels. *Anti-Dühring*, p. 25.

(3) Marx-Engels. *The Communist Manifesto*, Selected Works, Vol. I, p. 219 (International Publishers).

(4) Marx-Engels. Ibid., pp. 204-5.

(5) Marx. *Preface to Critique of Political Economy*, Selected Works, Vol. I, pp. 356-7.

(6) Engels. *Selected Correspondence of Marx and Engels*, p. 475.

(7) Marx. *The Eighteenth Brumaire* (International Publishers), p. 13.

(8) Plekhanov. *Essays in the History of Materialism*, p. 173.

(9) Lenin. *Karl Marx* (*Marx-Engels-Marxism*, p. 11).

CHAPTER FIVE

Problems that are dealt with in this chapter are to be found treated in many of the books previously referred to, especially in Engels' *Anti-Dühring*. A popular account of dialectical thinking is to be found in Levy's *Thinking* (Newnes). The most profound Marxist study of logic is contained in Lenin's *Notes on Hegel* (in *Philosophic Notebooks*) (available in German, but not in English).

(1) Lenin. *Notes on Hegel*.

(2) Engels. *Anti-Dühring*, p. 101.

(3) Lenin. *Materialism and Empirio-Criticism*, Selected Works, Vol. XI, pp. 198-9 (International Publishers).

(4) Lenin. *On Dialectics*, Selected Works, Vol. XI, p. 85.

(5) Marx-Engels. *The German Ideology* (Gesamt. Ausgabe, Vol. V, p. 110).*

(6) Marx-Engels. Ibid., p. 253. German edition.

* The section from which this is taken is not included in the English edition of *The German Ideology*.

(7) Plekhanov. *Dialectics and Logic* in *Fundamental Problems of Marxism.*

(8) Engels. *Anti-Dühring*, p. 148.

(9) Engels. Ibid., p. 31.

CHAPTER SIX

The attempt made in this chapter to expose some of the more flagrant examples of sophistry masquerading as dialectics should be regarded only as an introduction to T. A. Jackson's *Dialectics*, particularly to Chapter VII on the "Dialectic and its Critics," where MacMurray, Casey and the "Bloomsbury Marxists" are exhaustively analysed and refuted. Jackson examines the relations between Casey and Dietzgen and reaches the conclusion that "Casey has borrowed everything from Dietzgen—*except the materialism of his method.*"

(1) Lenin. *The Imperialist War.* Coll. Works, Vol. XVIII, p. 285 (International Publishers).

(2) Lenin. *On Dialectics*, Selected Works, Vol. XI, p. 82.

(3) Marx. *Selected Correspondence of Marx and Engels*, p. 252 (note).

(4) Lenin. Speech on the *Tax in Kind*, March 15, 1921. Selected Works, Vol. VIII, p. 107.

(5) Stalin. *Report to the Seventeenth Congress of the C.P.S.U.*, contained in *Socialism Victorious* (International Publishers), p. 27.

(6) Engels. *Selected Correspondence of Marx and Engels*, p. 295.

(7) Engels. Quoted, with some useful remarks in this connection, in Adoratsky's *Dialectical Materialism*, p. 61.

(8) Dimitroff. *The United Front*, p. 133 (International Publishers).

CHAPTER SEVEN

The special form which the age-long struggle between materialist and idealist philosophy assumed in the imperialist epoch was exhaustively studied by Lenin in his *Materialism and Empirio-Criticism.* This book is especially valuable for the English reader, since it unmasks the true nature of that compromising philosophy which has for so long dominated "advanced" thought in this country. It also develops positively many features of dialectical materialism, and deals in particular with the "revolution" in modern natural science (at that time radio-activity and the electron structure of matter had been discovered) which is shown to necessitate *dialectical* materialist, but by no means idealist, conclusions.

(1) Lenin. *Materialism and Empirio-Criticism*, Selected Works, XI, p. 391.

(2) Marx. *Poverty of Philosophy*, p. 107 (International Publishers).

(3) Lenin. *Materialism and Empirio-Criticism*, Selected Works, Vol. XI, p. 306.

CHAPTER EIGHT

For this chapter, with its varied subject-matter, we can only give a few of the most interesting references. The distorting effect of the division of labour on human beings, and its overcoming in the Socialist society, was a preoccupation of Marx from his earliest work onward (cf. *The German Ideology*, and *Capital*, Vol. I, Part 4.)

The class basis of morality is dealt with by Engels in *Anti-Dühring*, Part I, Chapter IX, *Morality and Law, Eternal Truths*. Writings of Lenin that deal with this particular question are available in *Marx-Engels-Marxism* and in *Lenin on Religion* (International Publishers).

For literature and art we can refer to Ralph Fox's *The Novel and the People* (International Publishers), Alick West's *Crisis and Criticism* (Lawrence and Wishart), and—a more profound study—Christopher Caudwell's *Illusion and Reality* (Macmillan); to the publications of the Critics' Group, which include Plekhanov's classic *Art and Society*, and to various periodicals, such as *International Literature* and *New Masses*.

(1) Levy. *Universe of Science*, p. 9 (Watts).

(2) *Literature of the Peoples of the U.S.S.R.*, V.O.K.S.

(3) Marx. *Critique of the Gotha Programme* (International Publishers, 1938 edition), p. 81.

(4) *Lenin on Religion* (International Publishers), p. 10.